# How to Buy
# A Home

# THE NO NONSENSE LIBRARY

## NO NONSENSE CAREER GUIDES

*Managing Time*
*No Nonsense Management*
*How to Choose a Career*
*How to Re-enter the Workforce*
*How to Write a Resume*
*No Nonsense Interviewing*
*Succeeding with Difficult People*

## NO NONSENSE FINANCIAL GUIDES

*How to Use Credit and Credit Cards*
*Investing in Mutual Funds*
*Investing in the Stock Market*
*Investing in Tax Free Bonds*
*Understanding Money Market Funds*
*Understanding IRA's*
*Understanding Treasury Bills and Other U.S. Government Securities*
*Understanding Common Stocks*
*Understanding Stock Options and Futures Markets*
*Understanding Social Security*
*Understanding Insurance*
*How to Plan and Invest for Your Retirement*
*Making a Will and Creating Estate Plans*

## NO NONSENSE REAL ESTATE GUIDES

*How to Buy a Home*
*Understanding Mortgages and Home Equity Loans*

## NO NONSENSE SUCCESS GUIDES

## NO NONSENSE HEALTH GUIDES

## NO NONSENSE COOKING GUIDES

## NO NONSENSE PARENTING GUIDES

## NO NONSENSE CAR GUIDES

# How to Buy
# A Home

## RUTH REJNIS

LONGMEADOW
PRESS

Published by Longmeadow Press, 201 High Ridge Road, Stamford, CT
06904.

*Cover design by Nancy Sabato*

*Interior design by Barbara Aronica*

ISBN: 0-681-41468-5

Printed in the United States of America

First Edition

0 9 8 7 6 5 4 3

# CONTENTS

— ∎ —

1  ∎ You *Can* Become a Homeowner!  1
2  ∎ Looking at Your Downpayment Choices  5
3  ∎ Some Other Sources of Help  9
4  ∎ Financing Options  13
5  ∎ Preparing to Apply for a Loan  20
6  ∎ Househunting with and Without an Agent  26
7  ∎ The Resale, or "Used," House  34
8  ∎ Buying a Fixer-Upper  43
9  ∎ Can You Swing a New-Development Home?  47
10 ∎ Choosing a Condo or Co-Op  53
11 ∎ Auctions and Distressed Properties  61
12 ∎ Finding the Land if You Want to Build  68
13 ∎ The Very Affordable Manufactured Home  74
14 ∎ House Inspections: When? By Whom? How Much?  77
15 ∎ Negotiating the Sales Price and Contract  83
16 ∎ The Closing  89
17 ∎ Selling Your First Home  93
   Glossary  99

# AUTHOR'S NOTE

Change occurs constantly in the real estate marketplace, even though certain principles of good investment remain timeless. No book, therefore, can stand in for advice regarding your own financial and lifestyle position obtained from a tax advisor, real estate agent, attorney, or other professional in your area. Much success and good fortune with your decisions!

# ONE

# You *Can* Become a Homeowner!

> The difficult we do immediately. The impossible takes a little longer.
> —Slogan of the U.S. Army Air Forces

Good words to househunt by!

You may feel that buying a home has become well out of your reach. The real estate market seems to you more and more perplexing and discouraging. But the material that follows can help you become a homeowner.

## If the Cards Seem Stacked Against You

With some work on your part, and a good deal of confidence, you *can* buy a home, even if

- you have saved only $2,000 and do not know where the rest of the money you need will come from;

- you feel sure your income is not high enough to qualify for a mortgage;

- you live in a part of the country where housing prices are very high;

- you have had credit problems in the past;

- you are back on good financial footing now, but you filed for bankruptcy just a couple of years ago; or

• you do not want a condominium, but are sure that is all you can afford.

## The Biggest Hurdle

Aside from prospective buyers' lack of confidence, the major stumbling block to homeownership today is not home prices, and not mortgage interest rates. It is the downpayment.

Is this your concern? There are many suggestions in this book that will help you find that elusive very large chunk of change.

## Being Realistic

First home and starter home are terms you have probably seen frequently in real estate articles that have convinced you that you cannot buy. But what you are looking for this time out is what is known as a foothold on the ownership ladder. Forget the dream house this time around. Maybe that will come two or three homes down the road. First-timers must make a lot of compromises.

Keep your eyes on one objective: buying a solid home that you will be able to sell when you want, probably in the next few years, and, it is hoped, with at least a slight profit. Consider *any* home that will help you achieve this goal.

## The Value of Ownership

Buying a home is still a good investment, no matter how sluggish the real estate market. Although nowadays you should be buying more for a decent place to live and fixed housing costs each month, not for the money-making appreciation, in the long run—and we are talking decades here—your first home will almost surely become the best investment you ever made.

In the short term, of course, your mortgage interest and real estate taxes are deductible from federal returns. The appreciation of your property might be slow, with some years of low inflation and a general economic malaise, but appreciate it will over the long haul. Market appreciation, and the equity you are also building by paying off a mortgage, are forced savings you almost certainly would not have if you did not own a home.

## The Buying Mindset

You will have to make some sacrifices, if you are not already doing so. Hold down the credit card purchases, put off buying the new car, and in general retrench and save. Keep the following points in mind:

• If you want to become even more serious about saving, dispense with the lavish wedding you have pictured, and have a smaller one, depositing the extra funds in your "house" account. Instead of an expensive honeymoon, opt for a budget-minded spot. Vacations, if taken at all, can also be downscaled. You have a goal here, and that's how the dollars add up.

• Do not forget the expenses that go along with homeowning. You will have to pay real estate taxes, water bills, and perhaps trash collection fees where you move. There will be monthly maintenance costs in a condominium or cooperative. There will be repairs for which you, and not a landlord, will be responsible.

• Single and want to buy? Consider buying half a house (or condominium) with a friend or relative. It is done frequently by those who cannot afford a house on their own, or do not want that much space to themselves. Have a lawyer draw up a contract between you and your co-owner, spelling out every detail of the ownership, from who is responsible for how much of the mortgage payment each month to what happens when one of you wants to sell.

You don't have to be single to buy with others. For example, if it is not already being sold as two separate units, a four-story city house can be split into two duplex apartments large enough for families.

Now on to that major challenge—the downpayment.

---

## Tips to Remember

• Think about homebuying all of the time, which means saving money and generally rearranging your priorities.

• Keep an open mind about downpayment suggestions, financing programs, and housing styles. Don't dismiss anything without thinking through its possibilities for you.

• Having a house can be costly. Be sure that you can afford the myriad expenses that go with homeownership.

---

# Looking at Your Downpayment Choices

Your best choice for a minimal downpayment is a government-backed financing program (see chapter 3), such as the Federal Housing Administration (FHA), that allows little money down. Still, even if you need only a modest cash outlay, you will have to come up with *some* money.

You can do it. If you can afford to carry a house once you own one, and you do have some money for that 3 to 5 percent of the mortgage that you will need for closing expenses, it makes more sense to buy now by tapping every source you can for a downpayment.

## Why So High These Days?

Housing prices rose so drastically in the 1980s that even a 10-percent downpayment on a $120,000 house means that you will need $12,000. Add to that lenders who have been requiring more money these days because of bad real estate loans during those roaring eighties and you now must often put down 15 or even 20 percent. Twenty percent of $120,000 means scraping together $24,000.

# If You Are in a Special Situation.

If you are self-employed, have a poor credit record, or are very young, you might have to come up with more than the bare-bones minimum a lender is requiring. You also might have to if you want to buy more house than you can comfortably carry each month.

## Think

First, look around to see if you are sitting on cash you had not considered. Do you have stocks to sell? A life insurance policy you can borrow against (remembering in your budget the payments to bring its value back up)? Do you have valuable silver or jewelry? What about tapping into retirement savings? Be careful here, though, of penalties and income taxes due to such money. Can you sell a car?

You could borrow what you need as a cash advance on your credit card. The downside to this strategy is that credit card interest rates are among the highest being charged in the lending business. If you borrow to your credit limit for a home, you will not have any advance available for emergencies. Another, more important negative: such borrowing will push up your debt load in relation to your gross monthly income, and these figures could prevent you from getting the mortgage you want—perhaps from getting any mortgage at all.

Are you thinking about a bank loan? Personal loans carry interest rates higher than mortgages. A personal loan will also increase your debt load.

Lenders often ask mortgage applicants to show proof that downpayment funds have been in a bank account for three to six months. (This is why liquidating assets should start early in your househunting.) They require this verification to be assured that the funds have not been borrowed. Money that has to be repaid can put additional financial pressure on the new homeowner.

# Can the Folks Help Out?

More than 20 percent of first-time buyers get some financial help with the downpayment from their parents or others. Can your parents afford to advance you the money you still need? Will the money be a loan or a gift?

Your folks can give you $10,000 per year per parent with no tax obligation. The gift is not taxable to you and has no negative tax consequences for them either (the gift is not deductible for income tax purposes). If you are married, each of your parents can also give your spouse $10,000. Recipients need not be relatives.

Lenders are more willing to offer a mortgage when there are no strings attached to the downpayment, as with a gift. If your parents can help you, the lender will probably ask them to sign a gift letter specifically stating that the money is a present and does not have to be repaid.

If their check represents a loan, lenders will factor in a repayment plan with your other financial obligations, and this will reduce the size of the loan they are willing to make. Indeed, some lenders will not make a loan if all of the buyer's downpayment is borrowed.

When lenders check borrowers' resources and see a sizable deposit just prior to purchasing a house, they can pretty well figure out the downpayment came from someone else. So try to deposit money as early as you can, and continue making deposits, even small ones, as frequently as you can.

However your folks decide to help you, they ought to seek the advice of an accountant before writing a check. There are ways they can structure gifts and loans to make them, if not advantageous, then at least a little less painful, IRS-wise.

## Tips to Remember

- Liquidate assets and deposit these monies in a bank account as soon as possible.

- If the folks are helping out, be sure that you confirm whether their contribution is a gift or a loan, to avoid misunderstandings later.

- All of you should consult an accountant to learn the most advantageous way of giving or lending money.

# THREE

# Some Other Sources
# of Help

The FHA, Federal Housing Administration, is a government agency under the umbrella of the U.S. Department of Housing and Urban Development (HUD). With an FHA-backed loan you can buy with downpayments of 5 percent or less. You will be required to pay FHA mortgage insurance, however, that will cost you 3.8 percent of the loan up front, with monthly payments of .5 percent. These rates went into effect in 1991, designed to cut back on the number of problem loans made by this agency.

If you qualify for a VA-backed loan from the U.S. Department of Veterans Affairs, you do not have to make any downpayment. These loans are available to veterans or widows or widowers of veterans who died of service-related injuries.

If you are looking to buy in a rural area, the Farmers Home Administration (FmHA) also offers lower-than-market downpayment requirements and mortgage interest rates. But be aware that there are some restrictions to these loans.

Then there are houses purchased through the Resolution Trust Corporation (RTC), which call for 3 percent down if financial need can be proven. This agency's formula for financial need is very liberal, however. There is more about buying RTC homes in Chapter 11.

Your real estate agent can help you with all of these programs, or you can call the regional office for each agency.

## Look to Your State

Another downpayment source: Every state offers some type of program for first-time homebuyers that features low downpayment requirements and lower-than-market interest rates. Money is available through bond programs, with the agency handling the program known as Mortgage Finance Housing, the Housing Finance Agency, or some similar name.

There may be income ceilings, and you will likely be restricted to certain areas of a city or town, but the program has made homeowners of hundreds of thousands of househunters over the last decade. Contact your Governor's Office for the name and phone number of the mortgage finance agency in your state.

## Private Mortgage Insurance (PMI)

This is a common expense for first-timers. PMI is an insurance policy offered by several companies nationwide that allows buyers to make downpayments of 10 percent or less. The premium can be up to 1 percent of the mortgage due at closing, with annual premiums thereafter about 0.5 percent of the loan. The insurance can be dropped at a point when the lender feels its investment is safe, usually after five to seven years. Many private insurance companies will finance the insurance premium along with your mortgage loan, but at a higher rate than if you paid for it separately.

## The 5-Percent Solution

There are still a few lenders around who will allow a fixed-rate mortgage (usually not an adjustable-rate loan) with just 5 percent down. In tough (for them) economic times, some developers of new-home communities will also advertise a 5-percent downpayment, one or two even *no* downpayment. Developers will also—again, in certain economic markets—offer houses and condominiums under a lease/purchase plan. GE Capital Mortgage Insurance Companies is offering 5-percent loans to those with a whistle-clean credit history. Call them at 1-800-876-4343.

## Lease/Purchase Programs

Renting that leads to buying can be an excellent path of homeownership, but do not waste your time trying to make such an arrangement work in a booming sellers' market. They will not need you.

Here is how this works. You rent a house or condominium, signing a contract that states that at the end of 6, 12, or 18 months you will be allowed to buy that property, at a price set at the signing of the contract. This protects you from ordinary price increases in the housing market each year. Another good feature: the sellers, who for the moment will be your landlords, allow you to apply some of your rent toward the purchase, which will go toward a downpayment. Naturally, there is a written agreement between all parties to spell out specifics. The lease/purchase also works with new-home developers who are so anxious to sell their properties that they do not mind renting them a while.

Be very sure that your contract stipulates whether you *can* buy at the end of a specified period of time, or whether you *must* buy. Option money is not refunded if you do not choose to buy.

## Equity Sharing

Whether you will find this workable depends on the condition of the real estate market where you intend to buy, and on the national economy. You need an investor, and no one outside your family is likely to want to help you unless the value of your home is increasing regularly.

Most commonly in shared equity deals, an investor (known as the owner-investor) puts up the downpayment and perhaps even the closing costs. The buyer (known as the owner-occupant) lives in the home, makes the monthly mortgage payments, and pays for maintenance. Both names are on the deed.

At the end of a specified period (usually five years), the home is sold. If you want to stay in the house, you can refinance the loan. From the proceeds of the sale, the owner-investor receives the original downpayment and any closing costs he or she paid. If there is a profit, the two parties split it. If there is no profit, the agreement might be extended another two or three years, but some investors do sell at a loss.

The Internal Revenue Service recognizes equity sharing, requiring a written contract between co-owners. You would want one anyway. Some lenders might require a higher downpayment here, and perhaps a higher interest rate and points. Your real estate agent or a real estate lawyer should be able to direct you to a company that will put together the equity sharing arrangement for you. It should cost you about $500.

## Tips to Remember

- Check federal and state government programs for low downpayment requirements.

- Be aware of the real estate market, both nationally and locally, so that you know how much bargaining power you have. Some programs that could benefit you will be no help at all in a lively sellers' market.

- Look carefully at mortgage insurance fees—both private insurance and insurance with FHA-backed loans. You will have to add this expense to the carrying costs of a home.

# Financing Options

It is wise not to begin serious househunting—where you really *will* buy what you like—until you know about mortgages, and in fact have been prequalified by a mortgage lender. Indeed, most real estate agents will hustle you off to a lender before showing you homes.

## Who Offers Mortgages?

A wide variety of sources: mutual savings banks and savings and loan associations, commercial banks, credit unions, finance companies (those affiliated with or wholly owned by large real estate agencies or franchises), government agencies, mortgage bankers (companies that qualify applicants, find the best available loans, fund the initial loan, and then sell to or place these loans with another lender or investor) mortgage brokers (a person or company who, for a fee, will find a lender), and homesellers.

Start with the bank that has your savings and/or checking accounts, because lenders do give preferential treatment to their long-time customers. However, shop around with at least half a dozen lenders. Terms vary, and a fraction of a percentage point in interest can save you thousands of dollars over the life of a mortgage.

## A Variety of Loans

There are government-backed loans and what is termed conventional loans, where there is no government agency involved. Here are the most popular choices.

THE FIXED-TERM, X-PERCENT LOAN. This has traditionally been the most popular. The life of the mortgage can be 15, 20, 25, or 30 years, at an interest rate that remains the same for the duration of the loan. A fixed-rate, 15-year term loan, for example, might carry a lower interest rate than a 30-year loan, but the monthly payments are higher because the principal is being paid off twice as fast.

THE ADJUSTABLE-RATE LOAN (ARM). with this financing, there is a "teaser" low interest rate at the outset of the mortgage that can be three or more points lower than a fixed-rate loan. But this figure can rise dramatically after the first year, and steadily thereafter.

The interest rate lenders charge for ARMs are pegged to an independent financial index they select. To protect homebuyers from large rate increases, most lenders set limits on the amount rates may fluctuate when it is time for a loan's interest rate to be determined. This is known as the adjustable rate cap. Be *sure* to ask about caps when you inquire about ARMS.

Under government-backed loans there are FHA- and VA-backed loans, the little-known FmHA-guaranteed financing for those buying homes in rural areas, and state mortgage-finance agency loans. A popular choice has been the FHA assumable loan. Buyers with poor credit or job histories can buy houses here if they can afford a downpayment equal to the amount of equity in the owner's house. There is no formal application process, and a substantial savings on closing costs, which are minimal here. Also assumable are VA-backed mortgages. Requirements are tightening here, however, and some assumables carry high interest rates and large chunks of equity.

## Balloon Mortgages

You will also come upon balloon mortgages, offered by some lenders. When you take over a balloon loan, you agree to make a given monthly payment, which will amortize your loan over, say, thirty years. You might pay interest only on the loan for a fixed amount of time—five, seven, ten, or any predetermined number of years. At the end of this period, the entire unpaid balance of the loan (which is usually almost all of it) becomes due and payable. In other words, pay up, refinance, or lose the property.

Balloon mortgages can keep monthly housing costs down if you plan to move well within the period of the balloon. Otherwise, be wary.

## Fixed Rate Versus ARM

If you plan to pull up stakes after just three or four years, you might want to choose the attractive initial rates of the ARM, so that you are gone from that house before the rate begins its upward spiral. Or you might choose the ARM if fixed-rate mortgages are carrying a high interest rate at the time you are buying.

If you intend to stay in the house for an indeterminate number of years, but certainly more than three or five, and if interest rates are low at the moment, your choice will probably be the fixed-rate loan. The longer you plan to live in your house, the more it makes sense to pay discount points to lower your interest rate (points are usually tax deductible).

## A Growing Trend

An increasing number of borrowers these days are opting for 15-year loans in place of the more traditional 30-year term, both to build equity faster and to save thousands of dollars in finance charges. These loans may be a little harder to secure than the 30-year terms because the monthly payments are higher, which translates into your having to earn more money to qualify for the mortgage. Payments are not 50-percent higher, however. They are usually only 20 to 30 percent above payments on a 30-year mortgage, because more of each monthly payment goes toward principal instead of interest.

## Seller Financing

Homesellers sometimes offer mortgages to buyers for a limited time—usually three to five years—whereupon the buyer secures more traditional, long-term financing. This is usually only workable in a buyer's market. Or when a seller is highly motivated to move quickly.

## More to Consider

Buying a fixer-upper? Be sure to check state (Mortgage Finance Agency) and federal government agencies (FHA, VA) to see if there is fix-up help available at the time you are buying. The FHA, for example, offers the excellent 203(k) program, where you can secure just one loan to finance both buying and rehabilitating a property.

A smart move: Buy a small paperback book that can go by a variety of names (such as Mortgage Payments or Mortgage Calculator Guide), is printed by a number of different publishers, costs about $2.00, and contains nothing but figures. Used by lenders and real estate agents, the book can be invaluable to houseshoppers. It can tell you just by running your finger across a page what a $100,000 mortgage will cost you each month if it is a 30-year loan at 9 percent, if it is a 15-year loan at 9 percent, and so on.

## What to Ask Lenders

When you make phone calls, have by your side a list of questions you want answered. Ask for the mortgage department, or a mortgage loan officer. You will want to ask the following:

- *What types of financing do you have available now?*

- *How long a term are you willing to offer for each type of loan?*

- *Can ARMs be converted to fixed-rate loans at some point?*

- *What guidelines do you use for loan qualifications?*

- *What is your minimum downpayment requirement for each type of loan?*

- *Do you charge points?*

- *Is there an application fee?* Remember that these are nonrefundable and cannot be applied to any other expense.

- *Is there a prepayment penalty on any of the loans?* This is important if you think you might be transferred and will have to move sooner than you plan.

- *Do you offer preferred customer benefits?*

- *How long will a mortgage decision take after an application is made?* Three to five weeks is common in a busy market, less in a slow one.

- *How long will a mortgage commitment be effective?* Some lenders will make a commitment for ninety days, with renewals available. Some will make commitments for up to six months, especially on new construction.

- *Does the interest rate remain constant on the loan commitment?* Some commitments will be for the interest rate prevailing at the time of closing, which can be somewhat risky for you in a time of fluctuating rates. The best deal: lenders who guarantee the "best" rate. If interest rates go up before your closing date, they will stay with the rate at which they made their commitment to you. If rates are down by your closing, your mortgage will be at the lower rate.

Getting a good interest rate locked in is a ticklish business but an important one. You can write for a free fourteen-page booklet titled *A Consumer's Guide to Mortgage Lock-Ins,* available from the

Federal Reserve Board at 20th and C Streets NE, Washington, DC 20551.

• *What's new?* Many leaders promote, from time to time, special mortgage plans for that institution only.

A cautionary note: Be sure that you are getting comparative quotes on the *same* loans. Institutions have many programs, some differing only slightly.

## How Much Can You Borrow?

For their protection, mortgage lenders will make certain that you borrow only what you can afford to repay. Ten or fifteen years ago, most lenders would go by the gross annual income formula. For example, if you made $30,000 a year, you could get a mortgage loan of $60,000. Today, lenders who still use that formula, and they are mostly small, hometown institutions, allow 2½ or even 3 times gross annual income.

Then there is the income to housing costs formula. In this qualification procedure, the anticipated housing expenses are computed. These include mortgage payment, real estate taxes, fire and catastrophe insurance, and mortgage insurance, if any. To qualify with many lenders, your total monthly figure for housing expenses must not exceed 28 percent of your gross monthly income (some lenders will go slightly higher). For example, if you gross $2,000 a month, your housing expenses should not exceed $560 a month.

Another criterion is the income to long-term debt payment formula. Rather than monthly housing costs alone, here, all of the borrower's long-term (ten months or more) debt payments are calculated. Included are car payments, large outstanding charge account balances, child support and alimony payments, and college loans. To qualify with most lenders, the total monthly payment for housing expenses *and* long-term debts should not exceed 36 to 39 percent of gross monthly income. These guidelines will give you 8 percent or more for debt other than housing expenses.

If your debt load is above 40 percent, you might try alternative brokers, where you could get financing at a rate higher than the prevailing interest rate. If your situation is temporary, you can refinance when the bills are cleared up. You will not want this, of course, if you see no end in sight to your indebtedness.

---

## Tips to Remember

- Owning is not like renting, in that you will not be allowed to choose anything you like. A mortgage lender, unlike a landlord, will be sure that you buy only what that institution thinks you can comfortably afford.

- Call several lenders so that you can compare mortgage terms. They are not all alike.

- Give some thought to how long you might stay in this house. This can help you choose a type of mortgage.

- Check government agencies' programs, which can be more favorable than conventional financing.

---

# Preparing to Apply for a Loan

Having a document from a lender stating that that institution will offer you a mortgage of X dollars will help you look like the serious buyer you are. Prequalifying, or being offered a "conditional" mortgage, is almost, but not quite, as good as an actual loan. The principal ingredient missing from the lender's file is still a signed contract for the house you want to buy. Once you have that in hand, you can be offered a true mortgage, if the lender considers the property a sound investment for that institution. Prepurchase commitments differ among lenders. The better programs are contingent only on a satisfactorily signed sales contract and lender appraisal. *You* do not have to do any more qualifying.

## The Paper Chase

Income, debt, downpayment, and a good credit report are the prime components lenders use as a gauge of creditworthiness. From this information they will come up with an amount they will lend you. Perhaps you will learn that you need to pay off some old bills, or clean up your credit, or save still more.

Not every lender will require all of the following papers. Also, it is a good idea to take the mortgage application form home with you, to give it the attention it warrants, and not fill it out at the lending institution.

## What You Will Need

· Assets. Your holdings such as stocks and bonds (if you have an account with a stock brokerage firm, include the most recent statement), IRAs, vested amounts in retirement plans, surrender value of life-insurance policies, cars, and so on. List current balances, names and addresses of institutions, and account numbers for each item.

· Debts. Make a list of your credit cards, auto loans, school loans, and other debts. Show the name of the organization that has extended credit to you, the address, your account number, the amount owed, and the monthly payments. If you can, pay off as many bills as possible to reduce your debt load.

· Divorce Documents. Collect the pertinent papers, which may be needed by the lender. You can elect to show alimony and/or child support papers to help you obtain the largest possible mortgage.

· Extra Income. If you have regular sources of extra income, add these to your application.

· Bankruptcy Statement. If you have experienced bankruptcy within the previous ten years, you must report it to the lender.

· Gift Letter. If mom and dad have helped you with the downpayment, be sure to have a letter from them attesting to the fact that the money is indeed a gift and not a loan.

· Income and Employment Records. Collect W-2 statements for the past two years and pay stubs from the previous month. This is not a good time to change jobs, unless the new position will be in the same line of work and you will be earning more money.

· Social Security Numbers. For you and anyone buying with you.

· Tax Returns. For the self-employed. You will need returns for the past two years.

· VA Documentation. If you are applying for a VA-backed loan, you will need a certificate of eligibility. To obtain this form, contact your local VA office six to eight weeks before applying for a loan.

# Your Credit Report

A vitally important element in being approved for a loan is what your credit report says about you. If you have no idea, it is wise to send for a copy now, before a lender sees it, so that you can clear up any errors.

Check the Yellow Pages under Credit Reporting Agencies to find the one that has you on file. You can expect to pay anywhere from $2 to $20 for a copy of your report. If you have recently been denied credit, there is no charge.

In this document you will find bill-paying information about you: When and how promptly you have paid credit cards, department store charges, auto loans, and the like. It is not, as many consumers mistakenly believe, a rating service. Credit bureaus attach no rating to those they list; they merely collect data and pass it on upon request.

Go over everything in the report carefully. If you see an error, work with the bureau—and the store, credit card company, or whoever made the mistake—until it is cleared up. Look into this at least a month before approaching a lender.

# Dealing with a Poor Credit History

Maybe you know your credit report will show delinquencies and difficulties you cannot fix because they are correct. So be prepared. Were you delinquent because you were laid off for a time? Had serious surgery? Perhaps a death in the family, or a divorce? You can send a letter of explanation to that effect to the credit bureau and ask them to affix it to your report to serve as an explanation for anyone requesting your file.

Offer this explanation to the mortgage loan officer. Copies of doctors' bills can help document long illnesses. If you had a dispute with a credit card company over a payment that is still being worked out in correspondence, bring copies of these letters with you to the lender.

## Some Options

If you have no explanation for delinquencies, you will just have to work around that black mark. You can explain to the mortgage loan officer that you are now more responsible about your debts or—your ace in the hole—that you can offer to make a larger downpayment than what would ordinarily be required.

Another suggestion: seller financing. Sellers often do not check buyers' creditworthiness because they feel they can always foreclose in the event of mortgage nonpayment. Or pick up an assumable loan that requires no qualifying at all.

You might also suggest a pledged account. This means the lending institution will have extra collateral available in case of your nonpayment. Funds supplied by you equal to three or four months of your mortgage payment are placed in a third-party account, perhaps with a title company. If you have no delinquencies for the first three years of the loan, this money, plus any interest accrued, will be returned to you. You can supply cash, or another type of collateral, such as stocks, bonds, or certificates of deposit.

The lease with an option to buy is another possible solution. You can build a good credit report with prompt rent payments. Finding a mortgage cosigner (who is likely to be mom and dad) is another consideration.

Finally, you can approach mortgage brokers, who apply for you to any number of lenders around the country. You will probably have to pay a somewhat higher interest rate, but if all goes well, you can refinance later. However, beware of interest rates approaching usury level that might be charged problem applicants. Shop around.

## Bankruptcy

If you can afford to buy a home now, do not let this credit blot stop you. Legally, there are no time limits on how soon you can secure a conventional mortgage after filing. Some lenders may turn you down no matter how far back the bankruptcy was, but others will lend within just one or two years. Here is what you must do in this instance:

- Do a lot of shopping around among lenders.

- Tell the truth about your situation, and appear apologetic and remorseful, not cavalier or casual.

- Explain what caused the bankruptcy.

- Have a scrupulously clean credit report since the bankruptcy. If you have charged nothing since then, you had better build up a credit record by charging inexpensive items or taking out small loans and then repaying them promptly. If a lender sees *no* repayment record, the institution will not know if you can now handle debt.

- Have a sizable downpayment.

- Use some of the buying options suggested earlier in this chapter.

When you have that prequalifying document, you are ready to begin serious househunting.

---

## Tips to Remember

- Prequalifying will ease your mind about what you can afford and will make you look better to a seller. Don't skip this step.

- Be prepared to explain any black marks or puzzling information in your credit or work histories.

- Have as much in liquid savings as you can muster when you are applying for a loan. The lender *will* check.

# Househunting with and Without an Agent

By all means take advantage of the many services offered by real estate agencies. They cost you nothing; it is the homeseller who pays the realty salesperson's fee.

The term *agent* will be used throughout this book, although, as you will note in the glossary, definitions vary among those working in realty offices.

## How an Agent Can Help

OFFERING FINANCING UPDATES. She (most residential agents are women) can apprise you of local lenders' policies and help you with prequalifying.

SUPPLYING LOCAL INFORMATION. Every real estate agent should know her territory well. Information on property taxes, schools, neighborhoods, recreation facilities, and so on, should be on the tip of her tongue.

DISPENSING PRINTED MATERIAL. If you ask, most realty people will offer you a street map of the area in which they sell, which will help you in driving around neighborhoods. Many local nonprofit organizations (the newcomers club, the library, the League of Women Voters) leave flyers and newsletters in real estate offices. They can also acquaint you with the community that interests you.

USING MULTIPLE LISTING SERVICE TOOLS. The orderly arrangement of listing sheets on nearly all of the property for sale in a given community—including price, pictures and all pertinent sales information—is the hallmark of Multiple Listing Services across the country. If you work with a real estate office that belongs to such a service, your househunt will be still less tiring—and a lot more thorough. Ask the real estate salesperson for the listing books. Go through the pictures to be sure that you are not missing anything.

OFFERING COMPARABLES. One of the best services a salesperson can provide is telling buyers at what price similar properties have recently sold. Ask to see the "comparables" book. These listings of houses that have sold within the past year, with both asking price and actual selling price shown on the page, should prevent you from overpaying.

EVALUATING PROPERTIES. You can expect your salesperson to have inspected a property before showing it to you, although this is not always possible with brand-new listings. She should be able to provide you with enough information about a house to keep you from trudging out to see what is definitely not for you.

## Disclosure

The primary area to which this term refers is real estate agents' disclosing to would-be buyers that they represent the seller. Many buyers do not know this. The seller pays the agent's commission from proceeds from the sale of the house. Agents' loyalties are with the seller, although they may be sincerely interested in helping you find a home you like.

Disclosure also requires that both agent and seller bring any problems with a house to the attention of buyers, hiding nothing. This can also apply to their knowledge of plans for the community, or the street where the house stands, that could also turn off a prospective buyer.

Just how much an agent—and to a greater extent, the seller—should disclose is still being weighed. In any event, you cannot afford to accept passively what agents say or don't say and then move on to the next buying stage. Poke around on your own until questions are answered to your satisfaction.

## Finding the Right Agent

If you are considering several towns, you will probably need a different agent for each, in that an agent's knowledge of her turf is one of the major benefits of her service. You will also want someone with whom you feel comfortable and whom you trust. Of course, you want a knowledgeable, hardworking person, too.

Ask for referrals from friends who have recently purchased a house. Take a look at the large display advertisements in your local paper, where real estate offices congratulate top sellers. These are obviously competent people. Call one of them and ask for an appointment. Attending open houses and talking with the agent on the premises is another strategy.

Two chancey methods: calling an office in response to an ad you have seen, and walking into an office and saying you want to buy a home. Most realty offices assign their agents floor time. Any prospect who comes in from the street during that time is the floor agent's customer. Unfortunately, floor time is not based on competence. A slight improvement on this move is asking for the listing agent for the property in the ad you have noted. This will at least direct you to the person who knows all about the house that interests you.

Skip part-timers. Also, if you feel the agent you have engaged is not doing the best job for you, find another. This is a major purchase and you need the best.

Finally, if you eventually buy a home not being sold through an agent, the person you have been working with receives no commission. Agents understand that's the way it goes sometimes.

# The Buyer's Broker

This is a small but growing trend: real estate agents who represent the homebuyer. Buyer's brokers can be particularly effective when acting for you in "for sale by owner" home sales.

These folks can represent buyers, or sellers and buyers at different times, or both parties at the same time. Go with "exclusive" agencies. Be sure that the broker you engage is working just for you.

Try to avoid signing an exclusive contract, which means that you cannot simultaneously work with other agents, and possibly that you may have to pay a commission to the buyer's broker even if you find a "for sale by owner" house. Ask the broker that interests you how he or she handles your finding a home on your own, if that should happen. Also try to limit the term of the contract, and ask for a thirty-day escape clause to give you an out if you are dissatisfied with the service.

Cost? You may be asked for a retainer of several hundred dollars, to be refunded when you purchase a home through that buyer's broker. You could be charged a flat fee, or there could be a 50-50 commission split between the seller's broker and your broker. You can negotiate for the lowest flat fee available, and then ask the seller to pay it; he or she expects to pay an agent's commission anyway. Or you could go with the commission and ask the seller to absorb this. All of this is negotiable.

There are still only a few buyer's brokers in many parts of the country. If you are interested, you can call toll-free the Buyers Resource, Consumer Advocate Division, located in Denver, at 1-800-359-4092 for the names and addresses of agents in your community.

Do you *need* a buyer's broker? You may well feel more

comfortable with one. Or you might feel you can work just as well with the typical real estate agent, who earns her commission from the seller. It's up to you.

## Discrimination

If you feel a real estate agent is steering you away from a home you want and can afford to buy because of race, marital status, children, sexual preference, and so on, you can (a) contact your local board of Realtors to lodge a complaint and/or (b) notify your state's real estate commission. Proven cases of discrimination can result in suspension or loss of license for the agent involved.

## Making the Househunt Easier

You will need some system to your search. First, be sure the agent knows what you want in a home. You will have discussed all of these details at home first, so that you can tell her you need three bedrooms, want to be on one floor, and so forth. This will help the agent and you, since you can immediately dismiss a number of unsuitable properties on the market.

Limit yourself to viewing no more than six to eight properties in one town in one day. Beyond this number, features will become blurred in your mind. Similary, give a day to each town if you are interested in several.

By all means drive around in the agent's car. Chauffeuring is also her business. While she is driving, you can take notes, mark your street map, or just take in the view. Following the agent in your own car is not a good idea. Being with her allows you to ask questions as they occur. You can always talk privately at home.

## Without an Agent

While you are driving around neighborhoods, you will notice several For Sale by Owner signs in front of properties that might also interest you. You might want to call these sellers and arrange to see the homes.

The biggest problem with "for sale by owner" homes—FSBOs—is overpricing.

When you call about FSBO ads, ask the price, and the street address, if you do not already know it. Let the seller talk about the number of rooms, special features, and the like. It is all right to give your name. The seller will feel more comfortable. If the house is one you have not seen, tell the seller you will call him or her back if you want to go through it.

Going through FSBOs can be awkward for both parties. Comment, if you like, on the attractively decorated master bedroom, but say nothing about the condition of the house, or the asking price, at this stage. Whatever you do, do not remark negatively on the sellers' taste in furnishings, or put down any extra touches they have added to their home. They will be insulted and you may do yourself out of a house. Emotions run high with FSBOs.

If you really like the house, call about a second visit. Take one of the computer printout sheets the real estate agent gave you about another property, and use that form to draw up questions for the FSBO house: size of the lot, age of the house, room dimensions, and so on. Still interested after seeing it again? See chapter 15 on negotiating.

## A Few Final Words

You cannot pass over to a real estate agent, even a buyer's broker, the total responsibility for finding you a perfect home and then making sure that you become its owner. It is you who must watch out for your money and your happiness, and you who must make the right decisions each step of the way along the buying process. *You're* in charge here!

# Tips to Remember

▪ Unless you engage a buyer's broker, remember that a real estate agent represents the home seller and her loyalty is with that party.

▪ Choose a fulltime agent, one who is knowledgeable about the community that interests you.

▪ Don't delegate full responsibility to the agent for finding you the home you want.

—  ·  —

# The Resale, or "Used," House

Odds are that this is the type of home you will buy simply because there are more of them than new houses, condominiums, or other housing styles. A resale house is any dwelling that has been previously owned, whether for six months or two hundred years.

## Pros

Resale homes are almost always in "finished," attractively land-scaped neighborhoods, without the stark, barren look of a new development. Also, houses of a certain vintage were sturdily constructed, with solid basements, thick plastic walls, and other materials that are not likely to be used these days because they are simply too expensive.

## The Flip Side

You might find an ancient heating system with an older home. Or the occasional design that seems dated rather than charmingly elderly. Or the expense of replacing old windows or adding proper insulation.

## Looking Around

*The most important factor to consider in buying a home is its location.* Keep this in mind in looking at *any* house. A poor house that needs work, but is in a good neighborhood, can be a good buy. A good house in a poor neighborhood is a bad investment. What you are more likely to buy is a house well suited to its surroundings.

## Revival Neighborhoods

There are enclaves in many cities and towns that are on the way *back* from decay and decline. These restoration neighborhoods can offer several blocks of houses in seemingly poor condition, but they are being bought and spruced up by back-to-the-city enthusiasts. They can be a good bargain that will repay the buyer well over the years.

## Old Versus New

Real estate professionals agree that new homes are not necessarily better buys than older homes. What determines the value of each, specialists say, is its *location*.

## Why Not?

Consider buying a two-family house and becoming a landlord. A rent check coming in each month can help very nicely with a mortgage payment, and lenders sometimes take that rent into account when evaluating mortgage applicants. Caution: some two-family houses are very costly these days, in that everyone else thinks this is a good idea, too. Rent controls, if they exist in your community, are another consideration.

# As You Househunt

Look for a home that is traditional for its neighborhood. A California ultracontemporary home in a community of two-story Colonials could bring you a long wait when you want to sell. Corporate transferees and military families know that buying the most ordinary house, one that will appeal to the widest pool of buyers, is best for those who move often.

You will, of course, check into commuting time where you are looking, as well as schools, houses of worship, and nearby shopping. Ask the seller or the real estate agent about any extra fees that go along with the house that interests you. Besides real estate taxes, these can be costs for trash pickup or curbside recycling, and fees for mandatory membership in a community association.

Be very sure that if you want to make any drastic changes to the appearance of the house that you will be able to do so according to that community's zoning laws. This could apply to a sunroom or greenhouse, constructing an extra bedroom or a garage, putting in an in-ground pool, and perhaps even a sturdy toolshed.

# The Exterior

Location is not the only factor that determines both satisfaction and investment appreciation. There are what are known as features in each home as well. Some are good, and some are a detriment.

How long you plan to stay in a home should determine how you rate what you see. If you expect to live there, say, ten years, you will be looking for comfort. If you plan to move perhaps after five years, you are likely to be more interested in investment potential (be wary of too-high expectations here).

## Desirable Features

• A breathtaking view (don't pay extra for it, unless it is water-front).

- Attached garage next to house, preferably with built-in shelving.

- Carport (in the South).

- Porch, deck and/or patio (screened-in is better than open).

- Self-insulating windows and sliding glass doors.

- Storm windows (in the South, no storms is acceptable).

- Back door leading to a mud room, or other storage area.

- Smoothly flowing traffic pattern.

- Kitchen window overlooking backyard (if you have small children).

- At least 1½ baths, with at least one bathtub in the house.

- Bathrooms with outside windows.

- Laundry facilities in a separate room near the kitchen.

- Plenty of closet and storage space.

- "Great" rooms—combination living/dining/kitchen area, or at least a family room in addition to the living room.

- Formal living room, out of the way of day-to-day traffic. Fireplace is a plus.

- Dining room—for whatever use the owner chooses.

- True attic, with stairway leading up to this space.

- Full basement, with built-in shelving.

## Not Popular, but Still Acceptable, Features

- Garages under the house (some homeowners complain about drafts in rooms above them).

- Detached garages in the North.

- Back doors that open directly into the kitchen.

- The basement rec room—passé.

- Bathrooms with no windows, just vent fans.

- Laundry facilities in the basement or garage.

## Negative Features

- Having to walk through one room to get to another, especially bedrooms.

- Back doors that open into a family room.

- Basement areas turned into bedrooms.

- Old kitchens with minimal storage and little unbroken counter space.

- Just one bathroom.

- Inadequate closet and other storage space.

- No laundry facilities or room for their installation.

- No family room, even if there is a dining room that can be converted into a family's casual living area.

## Community Associations

These days many single-family home developments have owners associations—much like condominium communities do—designed, essentially, to preserve property values. Covenants for these communities can say no satellite dishes, no colored blinds, shades, or curtains at the windows, and on and on.

In some developments, membership in the owners association is mandatory, with others it is optional. Most charge an annual fee, if only as a fund for newsletters and small purchases, or perhaps to keep the entrance professionally landscaped.

There are pros and cons to buying into a neighborhood governed by covenants. Some feel comfortable about their investment knowing that there are strictures, while others feel they are losing freedom of expression. It is up to you to decide whether such a community is for you. Always ask if there is an owners association where you are looking, and request a copy of the covenants *before* you buy.

## Inspections and Warranties

Sellers putting a resale home on the market might have an inspection conducted by a professional company, and then offer that report to the buyer. They may attach a one-year warranty with the report, a warranty that probably cost them $300 or more.

This is a good sales ploy. The seller is assuring the homebuyer that the house is, if not in excellent condition, at least covered for major repairs for twelve months or however long the warranty runs. The only cost the buyer will pay during this time will be the price of the service call.

It is true that having a plumber come in to replace a $2.39 widget for free will still cost you the $40 house call, but you could come up against far more costly repairs, where you stand to save many hundreds, maybe thousands, of dollars.

Some points to consider:

· Check exclusions. Warranties almost never cover structural elements, such as roof repairs.

· Look to see if there are limits on preexisting conditions.

· Is there an extra charge for nonstandard items, such as swimming pool equipment?

You can purchase your own warranty, of course. Chapter 14 covers house inspections in detail.

## Tips to Remember

· The most important consideration in buying any house is its location.

· Make a list of the features you must have in a home, those you would like, and the ones that are unnecessary and perhaps even undesirable.

· Try to avoid the most lavish home on the block. Best bet: poorest-looking house in an otherwise solid neighborhood (if it does not need too many expensive repairs).

· Most valuable rooms, resale-wise: up-to-date kitchens and baths.

# EIGHT

# Buying a Fixer-Upper

You can probably save money buying a house that needs some work if it doesn't need *too* much work; that is, no serious defects in the foundation, high-priced repairs needed to the working systems, or a major reshuffling of rooms necessary to create a workable traffic pattern. All of this work is expensive, but does not add to the market value of the house; it is only what the next buyer will *expect*. An exception might be investing in a new restoration neighborhood, where, with enough care (and funds), a dilapidated house can eventually be worth a lot of money.

## How Many Repairs?

You might seriously consider houses that need painting, landscaping, minor or medium-size repairs, or carpeting and other cosmetic improvements. Upgrading the kitchen and bathrooms can also be profitable when it comes to resale, and so will adding a second bathroom. Houses with potential look untended and slightly shabby, but not like bombed-out shells.

## Shopping

You will have to use your own judgment in determining how much fixing up you will be able to undertake, both emotionally and financially. Keep in mind:

- Prices for shabby properties might be almost as high where you are as prices for houses in better condition. It is important not to overpay for *any* house, especially one that needs a still greater financial investment.

- Remember location!

- Be creative as you go through homes. Knowing how to fix flaws that might have turned off other buyers to a basically sound property could bring you an excellent deal.

- As you consider specific fixer-uppers, make notes on repairs needed (a house inspector will do a more thorough job later, of course). Then take out your calculator when you return home and figure roughly how much you will need in repair costs. If you cannot estimate costs of some malfunction, at least list the problem, with a repair figure to be filled in later. Seeing a sizable list of wrongs could well turn you off buying a particular property.

- Who will do the repairs in the house you buy? It is most cost effective if the owners do most of the work themselves, perhaps calling the professionals only for electrical work, plumbing, and heating.

- Look into local zoning restrictions when you find a house that interests you. Be sure that you can renovate the way you want, particularly if you want to add an extension to the house.

- How much time can you devote to a renovation project with your work schedule? Consider your lifestyle in determining how grand a rehab project you can undertake.

- Historic districts bring special concerns. You may be restricted from making the types of changes you envision to the property that interests you.

- A house inspection makes good sense in buying any resale home. Here, it is vital.

# What Should You Pay?

Take the market value of the house (Chapter 15 explains how to determine this) and deduct what you think repairs will cost (adding a little in the event you lowballed this figure), and you should come up with a fair offer.

Another formula. How much would the house be worth if it were in top-grade condition? Let's say the asking price is $95,000. But it could bring $110,000 with some improvements. You should buy at 20 to 30 percent below what the house would cost if it were not a fixer-upper. So, 20 percent of $110,000 is $22,000. You might consider an offer of $88,000, or even lower, to start.

The sales contract should state "subject to the buyer obtaining a satisfactory inspection report and satisfactory repair bids within 10 business days." The first part of the phrase is standard these days; the second should be incorporated in fixer-upper bids.

# Financing Fixes

For rehab money:

▪ You can look into the federal government's 203(k) program (under HUD), whereby a mortgage and home improvement loan are combined in one package. Also, ask HUD about any regional or local rehab programs.

▪ There is also a relatively new financing service called the Community Home Improvement Mortgage Loan program, but it does have income limits for borrowers. Introduced by Fannie Mae and GE Capital Mortgage Insurance Companies, this program also lets buyers finance both the purchase of a home and its renovation in a single mortgage. There are income ceilings, and the program is so far available only in several major cities. Call GE Capital Mortgage Companies at 1-800-876-4343.

▪ Your state housing finance agency might have low-cost fix-up loans. Call your Governor's Office.

- See what your contractor has to offer in the way of loans. They sometimes offer financing, on terms that can be better or worse than you would find elsewhere, so continue to shop even after you get a contractor's quote on rates.

- Consider your credit union—always a good source of financing at attractive terms.

- Finally, you can apply for an unsecured home improvement loan with your local bank or savings and loan association. Terms and amounts that can be borrowed vary from one lender to another, but generally you can expect to be able to borrow as much as $15,000 or $20,000, for five or ten years, at a fairly high interest rate, usually a point or two above the current rate. With these loans, the lender may well want to see three written estimates for the work you want done.

## Tips to Remember

- Be very sure that the fixer-upper you want is worth salvaging! A house inspector can help you calculate repair costs.

- The best houses look shabby, need painting, landscaping, minor or medium-size repairs, perhaps kitchen and/or bath upgrading. Avoid those calling for major repairs.

- To save money, do as much of the fix-up work as you can yourself.

- Can you afford a monthly mortgage payment and a sizable home improvement loan?

— • —

# NINE

# Can You Swing a New-Development Home?

Is this your dream? Brand-new houses and tight budgets do not seem to belong in the same sentence. But it might be possible for you to purchase a new house in a development. Unless you and your family are in the construction trades, having a new custom-designed and built house is probably out of the question. We are talking about single-family homes here. More than likely you *can* find affordable new condominiums and townhomes in your price range.

Perhaps your home will be built right on the site, but more likely it will be a manufactured home. There is more about this type of housing in Chapter 13.

## The Brand-New Affordables

You will get a better buy on homes way out beyond the suburbs, where the developer has not had to pay an exorbitant price for the land. Just make sure the location is not too far from services and amenities if convenience is important to you.

Look for the innovative builders in your area who specialize in *quality* medium-cost construction. You might call your state builders' association, probably located in the state capital, to see who builds mid-cost new homes in your area.

## Negotiating a Sweet Deal

You can bargain over the price of a new home just as you would in buying a resale house. Developers do not usually like to lower sales prices because this will cut the appraised value of future home sales in that particular development. However, the state of the economy, both national and local, the developer's finances, and other factors could make him quite amenable to "talking."

Sometimes you will see advertisements in the paper or banners running across a development's sales office announcing: Prices Slashed for Last Three Homes. When a community is essentially finished, a developer may want to "close out" the complex as quickly as possible. If there are two or three houses that remain stubbornly unsold, he might lower their price.

The developer who has many unsold homes is also likely to be amenable to a little negotiating. It costs money to carry empty houses. You will also be very welcome in the off-season for homebuying. The trick is to keep cool. Your attitude should be, "We like this house, of course, but we like others, too. Why should we buy yours?"

More likely than a price cut is negotiating with the developer over what will be included in a sales price that stays firm. Extras can be upgrades on the carpeting or appliances, draperies thrown into the deal, wallpapered rooms like the models, and so on. You can also ask that the developer help with the closing costs, delay the closing if that is more convenient for you, or any other detail *you* find important.

Be careful with frills. If the builder offers you, say, a $5,000 price cut or a similar amount to be used to buy furnishings from the company's design center, choose the money. There is often quite a markup on developers' upgrades.

One note of caution: In a very hot seller's market, or in an already low-priced, new-home community for which folks are standing in line to buy, you do not hold much of a hand for bargaining. You have to know your market.

# Buying Before It's Built

You will often see advertisements with headlines like these: Pre-Construction Prices Through September 15; Pre-Construction Prices for Phase II of Pheasant Run. Is this just another sales come-on?

Obviously, a preconstruction price is the first price at which a new development house is offered. Developers concede that they underprice a little at the beginning to get the ball rolling. How much can you save? Houses sold when the development is complete can be 20 to 30 percent more than the price of preconstruction homes! Assuming that you can wait for your home to be built and that the builder is reputable, this can be a very good deal for you.

One problem: uncertainty about when you will actually have the house. Sometimes there are construction delays and delivery snags, and if you need to get into your new home *now*, you can become a nervous wreck. Of course you *will* have a lower price that is locked in.

Buying early also gives you a choice of location; you do not have to take what's left. Preconstruction prices almost always begin an upward spiral, sometimes only weeks after the development is considered open.

# Checklist

· Know your builder. You can't really judge a development from a color brochure or diorama in the sales office.

· If you are one of the early buyers in a new-home community, will you be able to accept living virtually alone until more people move in? Will you be able to drive around the development in bad weather? Can you handle construction noise?

· You will want to add a paragraph to your contract stating that there will be no design changes or switches in any materials used on your house without your written approval. To make sure that your house is the same as the model, get a copy of the blueprints and specifications and have them become a part of the contract.

- You might want to have an architect review all of the material in your contract, including blueprints and specs, of course, to be sure that there are no hidden design problems or serious faults, such as with the foundation. Naturally, you will not hire the developer's architect or anyone he suggests.

- Concerned about delivery delay? You can ask for a clause in the contract requiring the builder to notify you two months in advance of the completion date.

- If you are buying a small home and are already considering expanding it, be sure that you can do so following local regulations and according to covenants of the new-home community.

## Downpayment and Financing Help

Some developers do all they can to help you buy, including shaving downpayment requirements to as low as 5 percent and offering financing at attractive rates. They are able to do this through their relationship with the bank or other lender who is handling the financing for the project.

By all means jot down all of the information a developer offers about mortgage loans and interest rates. Then do some comparison shopping.

## Checking It Out

There will be an initial walk-through of your new home, at which time you have a chance to assure yourself that the builder has completed the job to your satisfaction. Anything that has not been completed or is not up to standard should be jotted down on what is known as a punch list. Ask the builder to fix all of the problems on your punch list before the closing. Then make a final inspection to see that all of these items have been resolved.

Sometimes the builder may contest a complaint. If a problem remains unresolved as closing nears, you can defer the closing until all of the questionable points have been cleared up. If the builder offers you cash instead of repairs, decline and ask for the repairs. They could cost more than the cash allowance he will make to you. Remember that *you* hold all of the cards before the closing. If ever there is a time to get the corrections you want, this is it.

What to check? What is on the punch list—and anything it does not cover. If you have any doubt about your ability to take such a microscopic look at a new house, you might want to engage a house inspector to go along with you. There is more about inspections in Chapter 14.

## Warranties

You will probably be offered a builder's warranty against problems with your new house. This is a one-year protection plan, not backed by an independent warrantor, which will cover the house against structural defects and malfunctions of the working systems. But if your builder is no longer around later, for one reason or another, you will be out of luck and your chances of being reimbursed for repairs you have made will be practically nonexistent.

However, if your house is covered by an insured warranty, you are, shall we say, home free. These plans are usually ten-year policies written by an independent warrantor, such as Home Owners Warranty (HOW). If anything goes awry with your builder, your claim, if considered a legitimate one, will be honored by the warrantor.

Try to secure an insured warranty from your developer. You can use his payment of an insured-policy premium as a negotiating tool. In the event he firmly refuses, you ought to purchase a policy of your own. A few hundred dollars is little to pay to ensure the proper functioning of an investment of many, many times that figure.

# Tips to Remember

· You can negotiate—over price and extras—in a new-home community the same way you can in buying a resale house. Bargain as much as you can, especially in a slow market.

· Besides location, the reputation of the developer is vital to a successful new-home community.

· Ask the developer for an insured warranty. If he says no, purchase the policy yourself.

# Choosing a Condo or Co-Op

With one of these home styles you could save $10–30,000—or more—over the price of a single-family house comprising the same space. You can also frequently enjoy a swimming pool, tennis courts, fitness center, and clubhouse right on the grounds of your complex.

And, as a first-time buyer, you will probably be able to live in a better location with a condo than you would if you purchased a traditional, resale single-family home. This is because there are so many others along with you sharing the expense for the land-scaping and amenities you enjoy. Condos also offer the attraction of low maintenance. They have, in fact, made homeowners out of millions of entry-level househunters who might otherwise still be renting.

## Terms of Enlightenment

TOWNHOME. A two-story attached unit with the sleeping quarters upstairs. It may be run in a joint-ownership style, the way the condo is, or residents could own their own plot of land, as well as everything associated with the home, such as the roof and exterior walls.

PATIO HOMES. The opposite of a townhome in that it is a one-floor unit with a patio or deck in the rear. Owners generally buy own their own unit, plus the land under and around it (their front and back yards).

COOPERATIVE. A form of legal ownership and not an architectural style. In a co-op, tenants own their building by purchasing shares in it and forming a corporation to pay for maintenance and repairs.

CONDOMINIUM. The most popular of apartment ownership styles. Most of this chapter will discuss condos. If, however, you prefer townhomes or patio homes, by all means continue reading. The chapter can benefit you, as well.

## How Condos Work

This is a housing style almost totally dissimilar from single-family home ownership. One- and two-story garden complexes can be condos. A huge single-family house can be split into three living units and run as a condo. It is not an architectural style that determines a condo, but the legal system of ownership.

A condominium complex is a shared-ownership community. Residents own their own apartments, or units, and a proportional share of what is known as the common areas. These are the driveway leading to the complex, including its landscaping; carports or garages, if they exist; and all of the land outside each unit, including the bushes just under each window. If there are recreational amenities, these, too, are held jointly by owners.

Your mortgage interest is tax deductible, and so are the real estate taxes for your unit. You are also allowed a tax deduction for your share of real estate taxes on the common areas. You will know this amount from a statement sent to you by the owners' association. The monthly maintenance fee cannot be deducted.

## What "Togetherness" Entails

Every new condo buyer must join the association that "runs" the community, and pay a monthly fee to this association, which is run by a volunteer board of directors elected from among residents. Your dues, which can range anywhere from $50 to several hundred dollars a month, cover your share of the community's real estate taxes, insurance on the common areas, the cost of landscaping, and other joint expenses. Naturally, the fancier a place looks, the more it costs to run and the more you will have to pay each month to keep it going.

## Bylaws; Conditions, Covenants, and Restrictions (CC&Rs); and Rules and Regulations

There is a lot in writing to plow through when purchasing a condo. Each condominium community has its own rulings governing virtually every aspect of life within the community (but outside your own four walls). Read everything, or have your lawyer read, and ask him to check special points that are of concern to you.

If you plan to install a lime-green awning over your front door, for example, you will probably not be allowed. You could be restricted from having a bird bath on your front lawn. None of this may bother *you*, but it annoys some folks, particularly those who have owned their own homes and are not used to restrictions.

More seriously, a condominium association's rulings may state no pets, and you have one or two. Or no home business where there is traffic from the people you are serving. This could put a crimp in your career plans.

You can sell a condo to anyone you choose, unlike the cooperative, where new buyers must have approval of the cooperative board.

## Who's in Charge?

You are, that's who. This can be one of the major adjustments for those who come from apartment life. There is no building manager or managing agent you can call when a faucet drips in your apartment. It is your problem, just as it would be if you owned a single-family home. Problems with the common areas, of course, are handled by the board of directors, or the property manager the association has hired to handle maintenance.

## Beware of Overbuilding

The most important point to take away from this chapter is the warning that condo buying can be almost disastrous in one situation. The huge amount of overbuilding of condo complexes in some parts of any town or city has brought a glut of units to the market. You have to be *very* careful that you do not buy in a saturated area, where it will be difficult to sell when you want to move on.

If you do choose to buy in a region rife with condos, be sure that the complex you select has *some* attraction the others don't. Is it close to the commuter train line, or conveniently downtown? Is it next door to the super-mall? Does it have an excellent reputation, making it always in demand?

Keep in mind that another problem with selling in an overbuilt area is that you will be competing with the developer, who can offer virtually anything to a buyer (e.g. paid closing costs or a year's free maintenance) or a brand-new unit.

## Profitability

Will buying a condo prove to be as sound an investment as a single-family house? In both cases, it depends on the location and condition of the home, but, generally speaking, the house is likely to have an edge. This is not to say that a condo is a poor investment, just that in many sections of the country condos have appreciated poorly, if at all, in the last several years and can take a long time to resell.

## The Financial Statement

Major repairs and improvements to a condo must be paid for by special assessments to the unit owners. It is important that a healthy condo community have a contingency fund for emergency expenses and a reserve for future improvements or repairs. A portion of each unit owner's maintenance fee should be put into such funds.

Read through the financial statement to see if there have been any recent special assessments. Ask members of the board and the management company if any major changes or repairs are being contemplated. How much are they likely to cost? What sum is being held in reserve for them? How much more will be raised through special assessments? You might want to pay an accountant to explain the financial end of a condo community to you.

Another consideration: Some communities begin looking slightly rundown because the association does not want to spend money on upkeep. Also keep an eye out for a tightwad approach to routine maintenance.

## About Tenants

Condominium units are frequently bought for investment purposes. Some condo communities have a high percentage of renters. Owners make the best occupants, however, because it is their money, pride, and hope for future appreciation of the unit that are on the line.

Before you buy a condo, ask a member of the board or a representative of the management company about the ratio of owner-residents to tenants. Too many owner-investors could sway important decisions at a unit owners' meeting, and, because they are not living there, vote against major improvements to the community.

## Getting Nosier

Drive around the complex that interests you at night to check lighting, and again in the morning to have a look at rush-hour traffic. Walk around the grounds and talk to at least three residents. They will probably be happy to chat about the good points of their community and about any problems and looming expenses. Is there a community newsletter lying around in the laundry room or on a clubhouse table? Help yourself. Read about the residents to get some idea whether this is a place where you will feel at home.

Condo owners' principal complaints seem to be in the area of poor soundproofing between units. Be aware of this in going through apartments. If there is no one upstairs or next door during your visits, come back in the evening when there are television sets and stereos going. If need be, go next door and ask the resident to turn on his or her television at normal sound. If you can hear noises from adjacent units, you'd be wise to keep on shopping.

## Buying into a New Community

Condos still under construction can, of course, offer the very latest in design features and amenities, and perhaps a good price. Still, caution is required here, too. Consider overbuilding and the reputation of the developer, and look closely at maintenance fees.

Builders occasionally lowball maintenance costs in new complexes. Sometimes this is done to attract buyers and sometimes it is because they do not know at that stage what maintenance actually will be. Sometimes, to lure buyers, developers advertise "no maintenance for two years." At the end of this period, however, maintenance costs my be set higher than residents dreamed. Be very clear on maintenance fees before buying into a new (uncompleted) complex.

Another point: recreational facilities are almost always the last part of a complex to be constructed. Sometimes the developer never gets around to them. Keep this in mind. Also, find out whether the pool, tennis courts, and so on will be free to residents, or if there will be an annual "recreation" charge for their use.

## For More Information

You can contact your state Department of Business Regulations or your state Board of Realtors for a "how to buy a condo" pamphlet, which most professional groups offer at no charge.

## Cooperatives

Not as common as condominiums, cooperatives are run totally differently. A cooperative apartment is considered personal property and not real estate. All of the unit owners in a cooperative building purchase shares in the corporation that owns and runs the co-op. When you buy your unit, you automatically become a co-owner and have a proprietary lease on your unit.

There is a monthly maintenance fee, which includes the same general charges that a condo owner pays, but co-op owners also pay their proportionate share of the building's mortgage, if there is one. The mortgage part of the monthly maintenance charge is tax deductible.

To buy a co-op apartment, you must be approved by the board of directors. So when you sell, of course, you must find a buyer likely to be given the green light by the board.

Because co-ops are considered personal, and not real, property, there is no mortgage if you want to buy. You obtain a secured co-op loan, the security being the certificates of your stock in the corporation. You can shop around for the best loan rates, which would, of course, include both fixed-and adjustable-rate packages. The interest on co-op loans is tax deductible.

## Which Is Better, Condo or Co-Op?

Both can be wise choices for a starter home, if chosen after careful preparation. The condo, however, because it is real estate and is owned free and clear without the strings of a corporation, comes out ahead. Regions of the country enter into this equation, though. In New York City, for example, where there are far more cooperatives than condominiums, the co-op is very attractive. However, in appreciation and ease of selling—again, depending on location—both would have to defer to the single-family house.

## Tips to Remember

- Beware of areas overbuilt with condo complexes.

- Check for soundproofing—the major complaint of owners.

- Be sure to talk with as many residents as you can in the complex that interests you.

- Go over carefully—or have your lawyer or accountant look closely at—all documents presented to you, especially financial statements.

- In a brand-new complex, where only a few units are open, be even more careful about buying. Look at the reputation of the builder.

- Also in brand-new communities, negotiate over price, upgrades to your unit, help with closing costs—anything.

# ELEVEN

# Auctions and Distressed Properties

Just a few years ago houses sold at auction were rare, or at least nowhere near as common as they have become in the last year or two. There have always been distressed properties, too, of course, but not nearly as many as have appeared since the late 1980s.

Today, auctions and distressed properties sales have become 'hot,' attracting more bidders than ever in their history. One program stands out above the others: the Resolution Trust Corporation.

## The RTC

You have probably seen those initials frequently in your local paper over the last two or three years. The Resolution Trust Corporation is a government-backed entity that is selling properties acquired from failed thrift associations.

Virtually every home held by the RTC is sold at auction. And are there bargains! Some houses have sold for $1,000! Admittedly, these are not in prime residential neighborhoods. And it should be pointed out, too, that other houses sell at market value. The better homes, naturally, have more bidders, which translates into higher prices. Still, there are many solid houses in attractive neighborhoods sold for what anyone would consider an excellent price. If the house is not a steal, the financing certainly is a bargain: low downpayment, no points, no closing costs.

Want to learn more? Here is a thumbnail picture of buying from the RTC.

PROPERTIES. Houses, condominiums, income-producing properties, hotels, stores, vacant land—all are sold by the RTC.

REGISTRATION. You must be preregistered in order to bid on any property, and in many cases in order to be in the room where bidding takes place.

QUALIFICATIONS. About half the properties sold at any one auction are considered conventional, which means that there are no income restrictions for bidders. The other half, called affordable, do carry income ceilings for participants.

PREVIEWING. You can walk through the properties coming up for bid. You would not want to bid on anything you have not seen!

UP-FRONT MONEY. On the day of the auction, you will need $1,000 or $500 (depending on your classification of conventional or affordable) to secure a bidder's card. You will hold up this card to the auctioneer when you want to make a bid. If your bid is successful, you pay—right then—the balance of either 3 percent for affordable homes or 10 percent for conventional.

MORTGAGE. For affordable housing, the federal government will provide a loan at market interest over thirty years, after a second credit check is concluded. Those buying conventional properties must supply financing, which can come from any lender they select.

BIDDER DEFAULT. If the highest bidder defaults for any reason, the second-highest bidder will be contacted, or the property will be put back on the block for the next auction.

REAL ESTATE AGENTS. If you are working with one, she can help you with RTC properties (her commission will be paid by that agency). You do not need an agent, however, to buy an RTC house.

For more information, call the RTC's toll-free information line: 1-800-782-3006.

## Properties Considered Distressed

These are houses and condominiums whose owners have defaulted in paying their mortgages, property taxes, or water bills. In the area of nonpayment of property taxes and water bills, you can contact your local tax collector, or other public official who conducts the tax sales, and ask about the next auction of these properties. You might, through a lawyer, contact the owners to see if you can buy the home from them before an auction.

There are a few points you should know, however. For one, owners sometimes manage to save their homes before auction time, but after their properties are publicly listed. Also, most houses have mortgages, and mortgage lenders do not allow *their* properties to go on the block for unpaid taxes. The lender will pay the taxes and then foreclose the property.

Also selling foreclosures: HUD, with its homes taken for nonpayment of FHA-backed loans. You see these homes advertised regularly, usually under a heading along the lines of "Own a HUD Home." The houses are sold through sealed bids, with financing arranged through a conventional mortgage lender and insured by the FHA. Downpayment requirements can be as low as $100 with some incentive programs.

Buyers can finance up to 100 percent of the closing costs, including the initial mortgage insurance premium required by the FHA. Buyers can ask HUD to pay some of the closing costs, and the agency will help with some repair costs. Caution: *many* of these homes need too much work for the budget-conscious.

For more information, call the HUD Homes Information System, toll-free, at 1-800-366-4582 *any time*.

Still more houses: The U.S. Department of Veterans Affairs has its list of VA foreclosures. And the Federal National Mortgage Corporation (Fannie Mae) has homes for sale *it* acquired through foreclosure. You can call Fannie Mae at 1-800-553-4636 weekdays during business hours.

## Lenders' Houses

Houses are also sold by banks that have taken them back for mortgage delinquencies and other nonpayments. You can contact the real estate owned, or REO, department of any bank and ask them for a list of their foreclosed properties.

## Any "Real" Bargains Here?

This depends on the number of other interested buyers; the desirability of a property in location, appearance, and upkeep; and on how close to market value the seller wants, or whether he or she is so eager to unload the property that the aim becomes one of taking virtually *any* money rather than waiting. Luck enters into these equations, too. If you do not walk away with a steal, you might do very well with a lower-than-usual downpayment, or some help with closing costs or mortgage financing.

## Keeping Cool at Any Auction

Homes sold through auction are sold *fast*, which is its principal attraction to sellers. It's fast for buyers, too.

Before attending an auction, you will have to do some homework. Acquire all of the printed material on the sale (known as a bidder's kit), and visit the homes that interest you. Auctions are conducted as each auction company sees fit. Some are very splashy, whereas others are simple affairs conducted on the front lawn of a home to be sold.

Some points to keep in mind:

• There are two golden rules at auctions. One is *caveat emptor*, or buyer beware. The second is *"as it is, where it is."* And it means just that. There are no refunds, exchanges, or adjustments at auctions.

• Be careful that you do not get so carried away by the adreneline-pumping proceedings that you overbid. Set a firm limit before the auction of your top offer for any property. You can arrive at that figure by comparison shopping at similar houses for sale in the nonauction arena.

• Once proceedings start, they move quickly. Pay *very* close attention, and hope the property you want is far into the proceedings so that you can become familiar with the auction process for a while.

• Be very sure that you are bidding on the property you want. With speed, mixups do occur.

• Be certain that the house you want will be delivered vacant. Government-sold properties usually are, but other sales might not be.

• Don't be shy. If you are afraid that you will not be able to speak up loudly, bring a friend who can do the bidding for you.

• Be very concerned that you will have clear title to the house.

• Be sure you know what *type* of auction you are attending. In an absolute auction, the seller requires no minimum bid, and the highest bidder automatically wins the right to purchase the property. These are the most desirable for buyers and tend to attract the largest crowd.

Another type is the minimum bid auction, where sellers agree to sell at the highest bid above an established minimum price. Minimum bid auctions can be good for buyers if the stated minimums are low enough. Bidding usually quickly surpasses the minimum, but once the minimum has been reached, the auction is absolute because the property is then sold to the highest bidder.

Sealed bid auctions require buyers to submit sealed bids by a set deadline. Afterward, they are opened and the highest-price bid is awarded the house. In a reserve auction, the seller reserves the right to accept or reject the highest bid. Obviously, this is not too appealing to buyers.

· There are many attendants in the auction room to help bidders. Ask them any questions you have.

· Ask in advance how the auction that interests you handles the actual buying of the homes. Some involve strictly cash sales.

With some auctions an on-site lender can offer you good financing terms because the institution expects to finance dozens, even hundreds, of homes sold during that sale. Ask about financing, of course, but shop around to see if you can better their mortgage package.

· Depending on where you live, you might have the right to cancel your purchase within a specified number of days following the sale.

Sold? Then head for the telephone to make some queries about upcoming events.

# Tips to Remember

- Do not bid on property you have not visited in advance of a sale.

- Remember that you are buying "as is."

- Compare values before bidding, so that you get a sense of the worth of the properties that interest you.

- Try for the best financing you can secure, the way you would with any home purchase.

- Keep rehabilitation costs in mind.

- Be prepared to close quickly. Speed is the reason for auctions.

# Finding the Land if You Want to Build

Building some styles of homes can be quite cost cutting. First, of course, comes finding the lot on which to build a house—or assemble the pieces.

## The Easier Way

If you already own a small plot of land, good for you! This immediately lowers your total homebuilding cost. Or perhaps you have a relative who owns some land he or she is not using and would like to sell—at a good price.

Or maybe your folks will join you in shopping for a lot that can be subdivided. You can build on yours; they can hold theirs or sell it to another would-be homebuilder.

Another thought: Does anyone in your family own a lot that could be split into two parcels, so that you could build on one? You will have to be very sure, however, that will work, zoning-wise.

## No Land

Buying land to have a house put on it will not work for you if you have to spend a lot of money for land before building. But if you live in a part of the country where land prices are still relatively inexpensive, it certainly can.

Remember, not all land is valuable. Some is barren and rocky, some is often hit by flash floods, and there are miles and miles of desert-like land broiling under the sun. Since you are on a budget, you probably cannot afford to buy in an established neighborhood, or perhaps even in farm country, where land is being sold to developers in parcels of thousands of acres apiece, if it is being sold at all.

## A Buyer's Checklist

- The first stop on your shopping schedule should be the Resolution Trust Corporation. The RTC sells vacant land, so you might be able to pick up a small parcel at a very good price. You can call this agency toll-free at 1-800-782-3006.

- Can this land be used as a homesite? What type of permit must be obtained? Is the lot large enough, according to local zoning laws, for construction of a home? How large a home? Check also whether the lot is too steep for building, and look at the land to be sure that it is level.

- Can you erect a manufactured home—your likely, most afford-able choice—on the lot? There are some municipalities with regulations against them.

- Is the lot you are considering serviced by public sewer and water?

- Be sure that you get clear title to the land.

- Do not forget resale value. Being plunked in the woods far from even the nearest hamlet might suit you fine, but when it comes time to sell, will you find a buyer with a similar preference?

## Financing

Many land sales are cash only. The most common means of financing is with the seller holding a short-term mortgage. Balloon loans are a possibility. You might be able to buy land on time through an installment land-purchase contract, whereby you agree to pay the seller the purchase price in installments over a period time. Title does not pass to you until you have made all payments, or at least a considerable number of them. Naturally, you will not build on land that you do not yet own.

Once you have an affordable, buildable lot, you are likely to choose an affordable manufactured home. They are discussed in the next chapter.

---

## Tips to Remember

▪ Not all land is valuable.

▪ Be sure that you can erect a house on the lot that interests you.

▪ Consider the resale value of the lot that interests you and the house you will erect on that land.

—  •  —

# The Very Affordable Manufactured Home

A manufactured home is likely to be your choice for a vacant parcel of land. It could also be your choice if you want a house that is already built, but which is less costly than those constructed entirely on a building site.

## "Manufactured" Explained

The new manufactured home communities you see in your area have been "built" entirely in a factory. They are produced in sections that can include even carpeting, and then shipped to the building site, where the parts are assembled to form a house. Often you cannot tell a manufactured home from one built brick-by-brick on the site.

They come in a variety of styles, from very plush to extremely simple. An average three-bedroom, two-bath, multisection manufactured home, loaded with amenities, will cost about $40,000 (including installation, but not including land). Larger houses can carry $100,000 price tags.

These houses must adhere to standards complying with a federal code set by HUD. Once called mobile homes, now, because they are permanent residences, the term is no longer used. This fact was recognized by the U.S. Congress in 1980 when it changed the name to manufactured homes in all of its federal laws and publications. The term mobile is still used in some older parks, however, and by some retailers who feel buyers still relate to the word.

## Where to Have Your Home

You can "build" on your lot—if the area you have in mind will permit manufactured homes according to local housing codes—or you can purchase an already built manufactured home in a new-home community. You can also buy a house from a dealer and have it put in a planned manufactured-home community.

Another option is buying a manufactured home and placing it in a rental community, where you lease the land beneath the house. You would have to look into this choice very carefully. Will you have a written lease for the land? For how long? How will the financing of your home work? How much are the utility hookup charges? What about the community's rules and regulations? Can you live with them?

Who handles maintenance? Are there special requirements when you want to sell? What if the owner of the community wants to sell his land? Will you then have to move your home? Will you be able to move it where you choose, or will local zoning laws deter you?

## Shopping

If you want to buy a home that is already assembled on its site, you can call your state manufactured homes association for the names of communities near you. The phone number of the nationwide association appears at the end of this chapter. They can help you find your local group.

If you own land and want to have a manufactured home put on your lot, you can contact one of the more than 100 companies nationwide that build these houses. They are represented by thousands of retailers around the country. The company you call can put you in touch with the retailer nearest you. Some manufacturers have their own sales centers in certain parts of the country, where you can also buy. The Manufactured Housing Institute, listed at the end of this chapter, can help you.

# Financing

If a manufactured home is permanently set on a foundation and is sold with land or erected on land owned by the new homeowner, it can usually be financed with a real estate mortgage. Mortgages can be secured from the same variety of lenders as any site-built home, including FHA and VA sources.

Manufactured homes on rented land and houses that are considered personal property rather than real estate (mobile homes come under this classification) are treated differently; they are not financed as real estate, with a home mortgage. Manufactured home retailers can arrange financing for these purchases, or you can shop around for better terms at banks and other lending institutions in your area, as well as government agencies such as FHA and VA.

# Mobile Homes

True mobile homes, erected before 1976 and usually situated in mobile home communities, are another housing option. Some of these "parks" are very attractive, and the homes in them can appreciate slightly in value rather than depreciate—the way the old single-width mobiles have in the past. We are not talking trailer camps here, but parks of usually double- and even triple-width units—homes that are almost never moved from their original site. If you are interested in mobiles, you do want to see some return on your investment so that you can use the money toward your next purchase. Shop carefully, and take heed of the suggestions made earlier for buying on rented land.

# For More Information

The Manufactured Housing Institute (MFI) can give you the phone number of your state group and can also help with manufacturers. Contact:

Manufactured Housing Institute
1745 Jefferson Davis Highway, Suite 511
Arlington, VA 22202
Telephone: (703) 979–6620

*How to Buy a Manufactured Home* is available for 50 cents from the Consumer Information Center, Dept. 429W, Pueblo, CO 81009.

---

## Tips to Remember

- Buy from a quality manufacturer.

- Keep an eye on resale potential. You want to come away from this purchase with at least some market appreciation to help toward the downpayment on your next home.

- Be sure that you can erect a manufactured home on the land you have.

# FOURTEEN

# House Inspections: When? By Whom? How Much?

The typical house inspection takes place in two stages: the first is the somewhat cursory look-over by you *before* you present an offer on a home, and the second is the more thorough job done by a home inspection service. This comes *after* you make your offer and it is accepted.

One of the contingencies for a sale to consider including in your contract to buy is a house inspection by anyone you designate. This is a common practice nowadays and a *very* sensible expenditure. House inspections cost from $150 to $500, with the average at $250, a small expense compared to an investment of perhaps $100,000 or more.

You do *not* have every house that interests you inspected. Call a professional only after you have made an offer to buy, the offer has been accepted, and you have signed a sales contract. It is rare for buyers to have more than one house inspection during the entire househunting experience.

The principal reason for a home inspection is to bring to light its flaws, problems that can give you room to negotiate over price. The second is to acquaint you with the workings of that particular dwelling. This is particularly important for the first-time buyer, who may know nothing of mechanical systems, roofs, and so on.

It is important that you never be so in love with a house that you cannot see its flaws. On the other hand, it is pointless to search for a home in mint condition. They are extremely rare. Just because a house needs work is no reason not to buy it—as long as you are aware of its defects and what they are likely to cost you, either immediately or a few years down the road.

## By Sellers

Especially in a very slow market for them, more and more sellers are offering prospective buyers home inspection reports they have ordered and paid for. If you are interested in a home that has such a report, good for you. You will save the expense of getting your own inspector, and you can take the report around the house with you to check points made by the inspector.

## When Inspecting

On your second, or even third, visit to a house that seriously interests you, you will want to get down to the nitty gritty. Don't worry, whatever you are checking will be gone over more thoroughly by the house inspector. What you are looking for here are any serious problems that will keep you from wasting time making a bid on the house, having an inspector over, and *then* learning about looming catastrophes.

Check the following:

- Look for major separations or extensive crumbling around the foundation (hairline cracks are usually no cause for alarm).

- Is there standing water in the basement or crawl space? If you are serious about the house, you might want to call an inspector at this point. Be wary of freshly painted walls and/or floors. Note, though, that sometimes dampness can be alleviated by a dehumidifier. Water in corners could be corrected by moving a downspout. Puddles should cause concern.

- Are there enough electrical outlets? Try all of the light switches. Check the doorbell. Having an electrical system upgraded is a somewhat major repair and hard to estimate cost-wise, but it is not something that should put you off a house.

* Get heating and cooling bills from the seller to give you an idea of what these expenses are likely to be.

* Look for sound plumbing by running faucets and flushing toilets and noting the water pressure. An inspector will check the condition of exposed pipes.

* Windows. Are there storms? Can you afford the high price of purchasing them?

* Floors. Are they even? What about the stairs?

* Are all of the appliances that will stay with the house in working order?

Read Chapter 7 for more spot-check tips.

## Calling the Pros

When you and the seller arrive at a sales price acceptable to both of you, you can have it written in the sales contract that the sale will proceed subject to a house inspection that proves satisfactory to you.

Now you call in someone who knows more about houses than you do. Perhaps you know a home remodeler in your town, or an engineer who does house inspections. Those folks can be fine, if you are very sure that they are qualified to look at *every* area of a house.

Be certain, too, they owe no allegiance to a real estate agency or company you might choose to do repair work. Your best bet: someone who has a contractor's license or experience in residential construction. Do not take a real estate agent's suggestion unless she supplies two or more names. If she mentions just one person, he or she may feel indebted to the agency.

You can also ask friends and business associates for referrals. Or call your mortgage lender or lawyer for recommendations.

There are large, nationwide inspection services, and local, one-person firms. Neither is especially better than the other. You can also look for those who are members of the American Society of Home Inspectors (ASHI), which sets professional standards for its members. Those who are not members—usually small, local services—should not necessarily be avoided.

## What to Ask an Inspection Company

Do they go on the roof and get into the crawl space under the house, if that is possible? Some do these checks as a matter of course, others will charge extra.

Testing for radon and asbestos, well-water contamination, or termites will usually cost you more than the flat fee. You might also be directed to someone else for these reports.

Ask what type of written report you can expect, and how quickly after the inspection. If possible, look at a sample report. Does it give the ages of specific systems in the house? Does it offer projections of when parts or systems might need repairs? Does it estimate the cost of these repairs and of remedies to existing problems? (Some of these questions you can get answers to by accompanying the inspector on his tour of the house.) Ask whether the inspection company carries any type of liability insurance to cover any damage to your house or major defects the house inspector does not catch.

The house inspector should not comment about the wisdom of your buying that particular house and you should not ask his advice. You might check your local Department of Consumer Affairs to see if any complaints have been lodged against the service you are thinking of using.

The Council of Better Business Bureaus offers a free booklet on tips on home inspections. You can call them at 703-276-0100.

## Condos and Co-Ops

You can use the foregoing information to look through the unit that interests you, and then call an inspection service to recheck the apartment *and* the basement and/or other common areas of the complex. The doors to these areas are usually locked. You will probably need permission for entry from the Board of Directors or the building superintendent or managing agent. Do not fail to make the extra effort, however.

Go along with the inspector. You may never see these areas again, but what you learn on your tour can help you put your unit into the larger framework of how the entire condo/co-op community works.

---

### Tips to Remember

• A professional house inspection is money well spent. Don't stint here.

• Avoid engaging anyone who offers to make repairs, or an inspector whose loyalty is apt to be with the seller or your real estate agency.

• No house is perfect. Just know how much imperfection you can live with—or afford to repair.

■ · ■

# FIFTEEN

# Negotiating a Sales Price and Contract

You *will* have to bargain over the price of the home you want. Never offer full price. Occasionally buyers offer *more* than the seller's asking price, although this occurs only in *very* lively sellers' markets.

## The First Step

First determine the fair market value of the house, which is defined as the highest price a ready, willing, and able buyer will pay and the lowest a ready, willing, and able seller will accept. You do this by comparing the property you want to buy with others in the same area that have been sold in the previous year. When you are ready to start negotiating, ask your realty agent to show you comparables (explained in Chapter 6). There you can check for homes similar to yours. What did they sell for? Were they larger than the one you want? Pretty much identical in size and features?

Next, compare what you determine is fair market value for the house with what the sellers are asking. Unless they have under-priced the house (and then you must ask yourself why), their price is likely to be higher than your evaluation price.

Why have they set the price that much higher? To allow room for negotiating? Because they have installed new carpeting? Take the position that sellers' upgrades do not always add to the resale value of a home.

## On Paper

It is wise to buy a small notebook at this point, and enter all of these figures for the house: asking price, prices of comparables, your ideal price (which would probably be a steal), your fair market estimate, and the absolute top-dollar price you would be willing to pay for the house.

Why would you pay a top-dollar price higher than fair market value, you ask? Because fair market value cannot be truly determined until the property is sold. During the negotiating process, it is still an estimate. Leave yourself a margin between your "steal" price and how high you would be willing to go, to allow for negotiating.

## Keeping Mum

During this stage, do not tell your real estate agent your top-dollar figure. Remember, the agent represents the seller. Tell her you will be willing to go up to $83,000 for that $85,000 house, and that is probably what you will wind up paying.

## Other Considerations

If it is a hot sellers' market, you will not have the bargaining power you would in a slow market. In a very trendy and popular neighborhood, you are also not likely to strike a bargain.

If the house you want has been on the market a long time, you are more likely to get your price or close to it. (Of course, you will ask yourself why it has been standing so long. Price too high and seller inflexible? Needs much work? Across the street from a filling station?)

Ask the agent if there have been any price reductions on the house you want to buy. This could indicate a very strong desire to sell and/or a rethinking of the property's value.

# Your Opening Bid, and Later Offers

Don't worry about making a bid that is too low. Real estate agents are required by law to present every reasonable offer to sellers. Depending on the condition of the house, bidding $90,000 for a property priced at $120,000 could be reasonable. Open with your best bid, but be willing to move up another $500 or $1,000 if the house really appeals to you. At the initial stage, ask for as few extras as possible. Be agreeable about the closing date.

How much below asking price should that initial offer be? The often-mentioned figure of 10 percent is really not accurate. There are too many variables, both in the economic picture in your region and the way sellers set prices for their homes. If you want a guideline, make that first offer 10 percent below your fair market value estimate, not the seller's asking price.

## Haggling

Your first offer will probably be refused. Sometimes the seller comes back with a counteroffer, but not usually. *He* does not want to give away his hand, either. Are you willing to go higher? If you raise your offer by $500, you might want to ask for some extras, such as the living room draperies. Still rejected? Offer another $1,000, and request a closing date most convenient for you.

At every stage of the bidding, mention to your real estate agent the negative aspects of the house, getting the point across to her that you are not so committed to it that you will pay *anything* to own it. The back-and-forth negotiating usually goes three rounds before an agreement is reached.

## The Contract

You must present a written offer to the seller. Your real estate agent will present you with a contract form to sign (short-form binders have become increasingly outdated).

This form will contain the date; your name and address, along with the seller's; the price you are offering for the home; a date for closing (which may be changed more than once); signatures of all parties involved; and the amount of the earnest money check you will be required to present as a token of your serious intent. This is usually a minimum of $500, but more often $1,000. Your check should be made out to the real estate agency's trust account, or to the firm that will be handling the closing. Never issue a check made out to the sellers.

The form is also likely to include how financing is to be arranged, mention of a termite inspection, and virtually every other detail connected with the sale. There is usually room on this form, which can run to two pages, for something called "additional terms, conditions, or addenda." Here is where you will fill in phrases calling for such things as your securing a mortgage satisfactory to you, a house inspection, the house being delivered vacant at the closing, and your inspection of the documents attached to buying a condominium or patio home.

You will also want a phrase along the lines of "subject to review [of the contract] by the buyer's attorney within three [or four] business days of signing the contract." This is important, whether you have a lawyer or not. If not, you can use the time to rethink your decision, and perhaps opt to back out.

## FSBOs

When there is no real estate agent involved, the same negotiating principles apply. After your second visit to the home you like—the call where you will poke around a bit more than you did on your initial visit—wait a day or two before making an offer in order to heighten the seller's anticipation.

To determine fair market value here, you can go through the computer-printout sheets you have secured from real estate agents for similar properties in the neighborhood. True, they will be what sellers are asking for their homes, not what they received, so they are not as valuable as comparables, but they will give you some idea of prices in the neighborhood.

Sitting down face to face with sellers is always difficult. Keep rational and friendly. Your offer hands them a quick sale, no more disruption in having a house on the market, and no sales commission to an agent. Still, they will not likely accept that first offer. Back you come with a second.

In the best possible scenario the buyer and seller will split the real estate commission. Of course, life rarely follows tidy scripts. The sellers may hold out for top dollar. Don't try to fight this. Write down your best offer, with your name, address, and phone number, and leave it with them. Tell them to call you if they change their minds, and continue househunting. You might want to keep in touch with them from time to time and ask how they are doing. If they come down in price a little, you might be willing to go up a little. That's how negotiating works.

Never give sellers an earnest money deposit. This check should be handed to your lawyer. All of the extras, such as closing dates and financing can be worked out with attorneys for both sides. You will definitely want a lawyer with an FSBO sale. Do *not* use the same legal counsel as the sellers.

## Engaging a Lawyer

It is a good idea for first-time buyers to have a lawyer, since this is such an unfamiliar process. That someone should be a real estate lawyer. Do not engage anyone who has another legal specialty. You call in a lawyer at the stage when you have bid on a property and need a professional to review the sales contract, covenants, bylaws, and the like.

How do you find one? Your real estate agent or mortgage lender will have some names. Or you can call your local bar association and ask for the names of lawyers specializing in local residential real estate.

Ask the individual you are considering if fees are at an hourly rate or whether there is a flat fee. You can expect to pay anywhere from $150 up. Lawyers' fees are not set according to any local or state formula. Shop around for the best terms, the way you would for any consumer purchase, and consider, of course, the reputation, knowledge, and experience of the lawyer you choose.

## Tips to Remember

- Do not let emotion get in the way of prudent, aggressive negotiation. This is especially important when dealing with FSBOs.

- Always keep to yourself the figure that represents the highest offer you will make on a particular house.

- Before making an offer, note the economic climate of your community, comparable sale prices of nearby homes, and how motivated the seller seems.

- Make your first offer low enough so that if it is snapped up you will not feel you have overpaid.

■ · ■

# SIXTEEN

# The Closing

After your mortgage has been approved you will be notified of the date of settlement, when the transfer of title takes place. However, in some parts of the country, particularly the West, there is an escrow, or settlement, agent. This individual handles the title transfer, and no one else need be present.

The transfer of property titles can be a confusing business for the average consumer. In fact, the government stepped in in 1974, with RESPA, the Real Estate Settlement Procedures Act, which now governs most of the steps in the transfer of property and protects the homebuyer with its disclosure requirements. Your real estate agent may offer you a copy of the RESPA booklet after your offer for a home has been accepted, or it may come from the lender with your loan package. If you do not see one, ask for a copy.

Keep in mind, too, that unless *everything* is paid at the closing, the property does not change hands. As soon as he or she knows, your lawyer should call and tell you what your closing expenses will be. You will likely be given a specific figure and told to bring to the closing a cashier's check in that amount. The money will be paid out in many different directions at that meeting. It would be wise to keep some money in your checking account, in the unlikely event something else pops up that can be paid by personal check.

Closing costs generally run 3 to 5 percent of the sale price of the home, so this can be a considerable expense. However, if you have bought a home with an assumable loan, you need pay only a few hundred dollars at settlement. You can expect to pay for such services as a title search and title insurance, a survey of the property, an appraisal fee, a mortgage processing fee, and a number of other charges. Ask about anything you do not understand. This is *your* money being spent!

## Homeowners Insurance

One payment you will be expected to make is a homeowners insurance premium, a policy always required by a mortgage lender, for the protection of that institution. You would want a policy, in any event.

Shop around for coverage the way you would for any other purchase. Rates and comprehensiveness vary. Some money-saving tips:

- Look first to the company that handles other insurance for you—car insurance, for example—and ask if they will offer a lower rate on homeowners insurance because you have other coverage with them.

- Ask whether discounts are offered if you have—or will install—such protective devices as smoke alarms and deadbolt locks.

- Opt for annual premiums, if you can, instead of monthly or quarterly, which frequently include a service charge.

- Choose the highest deductible you can, usually about $1,000. After all, the purpose of this insurance is to keep you from losing thousands of dollars with a major problem or catastrophe. You can probably pay the first $1,000 yourself.

## Is Anything Tax Deductible?

Unfortunately, not many closing expenses are. Your portion of any real estate taxes and interest paid in advance is tax deductible. Points are usually deductible. Your homeowners insurance premium is not. Save your itemized list of expenses paid at the closing to show your tax advisor. Most other closing costs are not deductible, but they might be added to your home's purchase price to arrive at its adjusted cost basis, so they do serve some tax purpose later.

Moving expenses? The majority are not deductible. Here, too, your accountant can advise you.

## More to Do

Arrange to have the electric and water meters read the morning of the closing, and then have an account established in your name. In dealing with your local water department you might have to make arrangements several weeks before the closing. Follow up to see that both have been done.

If the house is heated by oil, have the oil company measure what is left in the tank the day before closing, if that is agreeable to the seller. Sellers usually charge buyers for any sizable amount of remaining oil when title switches hands. If gas is the fuel, have the meter read on the day of the closing and an account opened in your name.

## The Walk-Through

Do it if you can on the morning of the closing. Make a list of any problems you find in the house that have occurred since the contract was signed and raise them at the closing. You might be able to get the seller to pay for repairs.

## And Then . . .

After the closing, make plans to celebrate, with lunch, dinner, or just a champagne toast. You have earned it!

Do follow up with phone calls in a week or two to your lawyer and/or real estate agent for material you did not receive at the closing. It will take four to six weeks for a copy of the recorded deed to be sent to you, but other documents should be forthcoming more quickly. Keep at it until your "house" file is complete.

# Tips to Remember

- Be sure that you understand each charge.

- Depending on how much leverage you have, and how much you have already won from the sellers, try bargaining still further with them over specific closing fees.

- Be sure to take a checkbook to the closing, in the event some money is needed to cover the unexpected.

# SEVENTEEN

# Selling Your First Home

Eventually you will probably want a larger home, or a fancier one. Maybe you will have a new job, and will want a less harried commute. In any event, you will decide to move. Now you will become a trade-up buyer, an expression you will hear frequently as you househunt *this* time.

## The Pluses

Each move from now on should build your estate and even, with luck, bring you closer to what you conceive as your dream house. There might be a few glitches here and there over the years, when the economy proves a stumbling block to your realizing the profit you thought you should have with one move or another, but overall your real estate career will likely be a profitable one. With some folks, their buying and selling houses has left them better fixed financially at retirement than the results of a lifetime of work. Virtually all homeowners congratulate themselves in the long term for making that initial real estate investment.

## What to Watch Out For

Don't move too soon after buying your first house. You should not sell before you have been in your home for three years, and four is better. Moving is expensive—and not just hiring the van and the other cash outlays attached to the physical hauling of a household from one point to another. Even more costly are the expenses connected with the transfer of property.

Three years is considered a reasonable point, when, if you do not make money on a house, you should not be losing several thousand dollars if you sell. Even a slight appreciation in the price of your home could help reimburse you for closing costs. If you move too soon, you will be *out* money.

Remember, you will probably have to pay a real estate agent's commission of 6 percent when selling your home. *And* you will need another 3 to 5 percent of purchase price for the closing costs on the next place you buy.

Three exceptions: (1) a neighborhood sinking into decline and you want to sell at the highest price you are likely to fetch for the place right now, (2) the unexpected corporate move—although you should not consider buying if you are frequently transferred—in which there is no question of your not going (but in this instance, your company is likely to see that you are not paying out of pocket), and (3) moving from a community or neighborhood where house prices have risen so dramatically, and the place has become so "hot," that you can take a tidy profit with you, even allowing for that battery of changing-homes expenses.

## Don't Move—Improve

If you are moving because you need more space, and are a bit regretful because you do like your present house and neighborhood, consider adding on the room(s) you need, local zoning laws permitting.

## The Corporate Transfer

Financially, this is the best way to move. Most companies offer to buy, at fair market value, the homes of employees who transfer or, in some cases, offer to lend them the equity in the house, without an interest charge, while the companies manage the property after the family moves out. Manage usually means maintaining the property and paying mortgage installments, insurance, and taxes until it is actually sold. Ask for as much help as you need. Your best choice for buying: an empty house, especially if the seller is another transferee as eager to get out as you are to get in.

## Juggling Finances

Your most important logistical problem is likely to be timing, in getting your equity from house 1 to make the downpayment on house 2. The best switch is to sign a contract to sell before you sign a contract to buy. Of course, once you accept an offer on the house you own, you are in a must-buy position, and have to choose from the properties available at the time.

If there is nothing you want to buy at the time, you can (a) refuse the offer or (b) accept it, but with a distant closing date of perhaps four to six months. The latter is a gamble, of course, but usually it is a safe bet. Just keep in mind that the buyer of your house can go to court to force a seller to close on his property in accordance with the contract, even if the seller has no place to go.

But what if the closing date on the house you have bought is two weeks away, you need the cash from the equity in house 1, and there is no buyer in sight? Or you have bought before you sold and are carrying two mortgages because you still have no buyer for your old house?

Some of the nation's largest real estate firms advertise from time to time to the effect, "list your house with us and we will guarantee it will be sold in ninety days, or we will buy it!" This is not as good a deal as it sounds. The price at which the real estate firm will buy your property is usually less than its market value. And you must still pay a real estate commission to the broker, even though she is also the new buyer.

## The Likely Solution

The bridge loan, also known as interim financing or a gap loan, is a commonly used, short-term, six-month mortgage, where you can draw out the equity on your old home for the downpayment and closing costs on a new one. Once you have sold house 1, you pay off your original mortgage and the bridge loan with the proceeds. Many different types of lenders write bridge loans at variable terms, so shop around.

## Renting an Unsold House

You might want to rent house 1 on a month-to-month basis, while continuing to allow real estate agents to show the property. You will have rental income to meet at least part of your mortgage payment. The house will also be occupied and maintained. Even if the furniture is not wildly attractive, a house shows better when furnished than when vacant. You can arrange for the tenant to handle the yard work, perhaps with a rent concession. You will not have to worry about vandalism, either, with an occupied house.

However, the tenants could perhaps be uncooperative with real estate agents. They could be untidy, and detract from the look of the house. There could be tax consequences to renting. Give renting careful thought, and by all means talk with your accountant first.

## The New-Development Home

Because trade-up buyers frequently have the "how do I sell my house in time to buy yours?" problem, developers offer a variety of plans to help the would-be buyer through this complication. Ask questions in the community that interests you.

# Eventually . . .

You *will* be settled in your second home, noting how familiar the transfer of property seemed this time around. Now you are knowledgeable and well prepared for your next adventure in the sell/buy marketplace!

---

## Tips to Remember

▪ Don't move too soon after buying your first home. You will lose money.

▪ Try not to buy your next home until you have a sales contract on your present house. You do not want to carry two mortgages.

▪ In a corporate transfer, ask for as much help as possible with selling your home.

---

# GLOSSARY

━━ ▪ ━━

*Amortization*. Prorated repayment of a debt. Most mortgages are being amortized every month that you make a payment to the lender.

*Appreciation*. The increase in value of real estate due to inflation and other economic factors.

*Assessment*. Tax or other charge levied on property by a taxing authority to pay for improvements such as sidewalks, streets, and sewers.

*Assumption of mortgage*. Buyer taking over seller's old mortgage, at the interest rate and terms of that original loan.

*Buy-down*. A temporary reduction in the interest rate on a loan by the lender in exchange for a fee paid in cash at the closing. It can lower monthly mortgage payments for, generally, two years, and can be paid for by the home seller, a developer, or any other willing party.

*Community associations*. Groups which one must, or may, join when buying into some developments. Even single-family home communities can form such associations.

*Contract*. An agreement between two parties. To be valid, a real estate contract must be dated, must be in writing, and must include a description of the property, the place and date of delivery of the deed, and all terms and conditions that were mutually agreed upon. It must also be signed by all parties concerned.

*Deed*. A written instrument that conveys title to real property.

*Default*. A breach of contract or failure to meet an obligation. Nonpayment of a mortgage beyond a certain number of payments is considered a default.

*Discount*. See *Points*.

*Equity*. The value an owner has in a piece of property exclusive of its mortgage and other liens. For example, if the market value of a house is $100,000, and the owner has paid off $5,000 of a $75,000 mortgage, the owner has $30,000 equity.

*Escrow*. Money or documents held by a third party until specific conditions of an agreement or contract are fulfilled.

*FmHA*. Farmers Home Administration, an agency of the U.S. Department of Agriculture that insures home loans in rural communities at favorable terms to qualified borrowers.

*FHA*. Federal Housing Administration, an agency created within HUD that insures mortgages on residential property, with downpayment requirements usually lower than those at the open market.

*Foreclosure*. Legal proceedings instigated by a lender to deprive a person of ownership rights when mortgage payments have not been kept up.

*FSBO* (pronounced fizbo). Stands for "for sale by owner," referring to homes being sold without the assistance of a real estate agency.

*HUD*. U.S. Department of Housing and Urban Development, from which most government housing programs emanate.

*Joint tenancy* (with right of survivorship). Property ownership by two or more persons with an undivided interest. If one owner dies, the property automatically passes to the other(s). Common with married couples.

*Leverage*. The effective use of money to buy property by using the smallest amount of one's own capital that is permitted, and borrowing as much as possible, in order to obtain the maximum percentage of return on the original investment.

*Lien*. A debt on a property; a mortgage, back taxes, or other claim.

*Market value*. Generally accepted as the highest price that a

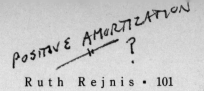
POSITIVE AMORTIZATION ?

ready, willing, and able buyer will pay and the lowest price a ready, willing, and able seller will accept for the property in question.

*Mortgagee*. The party or institution that lends the money.

*Mortgagor*. The person or persons that borrow the money, giving a lien on the property as security for the loan.

*Negative amortization*. The practice of *adding* to the principal of a loan when its monthly payments are insufficient to pay the interest due.

*Points*. Sometimes called discount. A fee that a lending institution charges for granting a mortgage. One point is 1 percent of the face value of the loan and is payable at the closing.

*Principal*. The amount of money borrowed; the amount of money still owed.

*Real estate broker*. Man or woman who has passed a state broker's test and represents others in realty transactions. Anyone having his or her own office must be a broker.

*Real estate salesperson*. Man or woman who has passed a state examination for this position and who works under the supervision of a broker.

*Realtor*. A real estate broker who is a member of the National Association of Realtors, a professional group. Not every broker is a Realtor (a trademark name owned by this association).

*Real estate taxes*. Levies on land and buildings charged to owners by local governing agencies. These charges, sometimes known as property taxes, are a primary source of local government revenues.

*Secondary mortgage market*. Quasi-governmental agencies such as the Federal National Mortgage Corporation (Fannie Mae) and the Federal Home Loan Mortgage Corporation (Freddie Mac) that purchase home loans from lenders and resell to investors, to keep mortgage money flowing to primary lenders.

*Tenancy in common*. Style of ownership in which two or more persons purchase a property jointly, but with no right of survivorship. They are free to will their share to anyone they choose, a principal difference between this form of ownership and joint tenancy. Used by friends or relatives buying together.

*Term.* The lifespan of a mortgage; 15 or 30 years, or any other period of time agreed upon by buyer and lender.

*Title.* Actual ownership; the right of possession and evidence of ownership.

*Title insurance.* An insurance policy that protects against any losses incurred because of defective title.

*Title search.* A professional examination of public records to determine the chain of ownership of a particular piece of property and to note any liens, mortgages, encumbrances, or other factors that might affect the title.

*Trust deed.* An instrument used in place of a mortgage in certain states; a third-party trustee, not the lender, holds the title to the property until the loan is paid out or defaulted.

*Variance.* An exception to a zoning ordinance granted to meet certain specified needs.

*Zoning.* Procedure that classifies real property for a number of different uses—residential, commercial, industrial, and so on—in accordance with a land-use plan. Ordinances are enforced by a local governing body.

# If you enjoyed this No Nonsense Guide you may want to order these other No Nonsense Financial Guides:

| Item No. | TITLE | PRICE |
|---|---|---|
| 681402474 | Understanding Stock Options & Futures Markets | 4.95 |
| 681402458 | How to Use Credit and Credit Cards | 4.50 |
| 681402369 | Understanding the Stock Market | 4.95 |
| 681402385 | Understanding Mutual Funds | 4.95 |
| 68140972X | Personal Banking | 4.50 |
| 681402431 | How to Choose a Discount Stockbroker | 4.50 |
| 681402377 | Understanding Common Stocks | 4.50 |
| 681402512 | Understanding IRA's | 4.50 |
| 681402393 | Understanding Money Market Funds | 4.50 |
| 681402423 | Understanding Treasury Bills and other U.S. Government Insurance | 4.50 |
| 681410493 | Understanding Insurance | 4.95 |
| 681410507 | Understanding Social Security | 4.95 |
| 681410485 | How to Plan and Invest for Your Retirement | 4.95 |

### Ordering is easy and convenient.
Order by phone with Visa, MasterCard, American Express or Discover:
☎ **1-800-322-2000,** Dept. 706
or send your order to:
Longmeadow Press, Order/Dept. 706,
P.O. Box 305188, Nashville, TN 37230-5188

Name _____

Address _____

City _____ State _____ Zip _____

| Item No. | Title | Qty | Total |
|---|---|---|---|
|  |  |  |  |
|  |  |  |  |
|  |  |  |  |
|  |  |  |  |

Check or Money Order enclosed Payable to Longmeadow Press

Charge: ☐ MasterCard ☐ VISA ☐ American Express ☐ Discover

Account Number

Card Expires

Signature _____ Date _____

| | Subtotal | |
|---|---|---|
| | Tax | |
| | Shipping | 2.95 |
| | Total | |

Please add your applicable sales tax: AK, DE, MT, MN, OR 0% – CO 3.6% – AL, GA, HI, IA, LA, ME, NE, VT, WY 4% – VA 4.5% – AR ID, IN, KS, KY, MA, MD, ME, NC, ND, OH, SC, SD, WI 5% – NM 5.25% – AZ 5.5% – MO 5.75% – DC, FL. MN, MS, NJ, NV PA, RI, WV 6% – CA, IL, UT 6.25% – NY, OK, TN, TX 7% – WA 7.5% – CT 8%

# If you enjoyed this No Nonsense Guide you may want to order these other No Nonsense Career Guides:

| ITEM No. | TITLE | PR |
|----------|-------|-----|
| 0681414049 | How To Use Your Time Wisely | 4. |
| 0681414030 | Managing People At Work | 4 |
| 0681401419 | No Nonsense Interviewing | 4. |
| 0681410477 | How To Write a Resume | 4. |
| 0681410450 | How To Choose a Career | 4. |
| 0681413891 | How to Re-enter The Work Force | 4. |

Ordering is easy and convenient.

Order by phone with Visa, MasterCard, American Express or Discov

☎ **1-800-322-2000,** Dept. 706

or send your order to:

Longmeadow Press, Order/Dept. 706,
P.O. Box 305188, Nashville, TN 37230-5188

Name _____

Address _____

City _____ State _____ Zip _____

| Item No. | Title | Qty | Total |
|----------|-------|-----|-------|
|  |  |  |  |
|  |  |  |  |
|  |  |  |  |
|  |  |  |  |

Check or Money Order enclosed Payable to Longmeadow Press

Charge: ☐ MasterCard ☐ VISA ☐ American Express ☐ Discover

Account Number

☐☐☐☐ ☐☐☐☐☐ ☐☐☐☐☐ ☐☐☐☐☐

| | |
|---|---|
| Subtotal | |
| Tax | |
| Shipping | 2.95 |
| Total | |

Card Expires

☐☐☐☐

Signature _____ Date _____

Please add your applicable sales tax: AK, DE, MT, MN, OR 0% – CO 3.6% – AL, GA, HI, IA, LA, ME, NE, VT, WY 4
VA 4.5% – AR ID, IN, KS, KY, MA, MD, ME, NC, ND, OH, SC, SD, WI 5% – NM 5.25% – AZ 5.5% – MO 5.75% –
DC, FL. MN, MS, NJ, NV PA, RI, WV 6% – CA, IL, UT 6.25% – NY, OK, TN, TX 7% – WA 7.5% – CT 8%

**Item No.     ITEM NO.**